THE 90% RULE:

HOW TO GET OUT OF DEBT AND PROSPER, AND WHY IT'S IMPORTANT

THE BIBLICAL METHOD FOR DEBT ELIMINATION AND WEALTH ACCUMULATION

Matthew M. Carter II

THE 90% RULE:

HOW TO GET OUT OF DEBT

AND PROSPER, AND WHY IT'S IMPORTANT

By

Matthew M. Carter II
Tallahassee, FL

The 90% Rule: How To Get Out Of Debt And Prosper And Why It's Important

Printed in the United States of America

Matthew M. Carter II
1904 Miccosukee Road
Unit 6
Tallahassee, Florida 32308

CONTENTS

Affirmation for Wealth

I am in a wealthy place!

Whatever God did for Abraham, He will do for me because of His promise!

I'm out of debt, my needs are met.

I have plenty more to put in store!

I am in a wealthy place!

In the name of Jesus Christ, I will never be broke another day in my life!

The Tithe belongs to God.

The rest belongs to me.

I am anointed with the wealth favor of God – NOW!

INTRODUCTION

During the last decade, Americans have done poorly and done well, economically speaking. As Dickens said, "It was the best of times; it was the worst of times." Unemployment in the United States is now at its highest level in 21 years with more than 3.7 million jobless. In 2001, the airline industry alone lost more than $5 billion. The holiday season, its busiest time of year, saw 65% fewer passengers. Savings and loans, and bank failures reached all-time highs. Those financial institutions that remained were merged with or bought out by others.

Forty million Americans cannot get credit cards, and of those who have them, five million have trouble making the payments. The American dream of owning a home has become a nightmare for millions of people. Insurance companies and employee pension funds (in all major industries) have gone bankrupt in record numbers. Millions of well-paying jobs in the United States have been lost through downsizing or exported to foreign countries. Individual consumer debts (credit card, installment, etc.) are higher than ever. The rich got richer and the poor got poorer!

It is against this backdrop that I have been telling individuals, church congregations and community organizations in urban and rural areas it's time for a change! It is time to realize that Christians are not supposed to be poor, broke and hungry. I believe the Apostle James when he said, "*Faith without works is dead*" (James 2:18). In essence, positive thinking will go only as far as positive action takes it. It takes a recognition that we must act upon our faith, recognizing that God will grant us the desires of our hearts. As a minister of the Gospel, I must give people hope. I must also give people an understanding of how to live a more complete life. By standing on God's Word, by faith, people will be moved by positive spiritual action.

Therefore, I have written **The 90% Rule: How to Get Out of Debt and Prosper and Why It's Important**. For short, I call it **The 90% Rule**. For more than thirty years, I have worked in the areas of personal and business finance – as a financial consultant, marketing professional, stockbroker and a business lawyer. Whether it was a corporation or an individual, my goal was to help them reduce their debts, increase their income and build wealth.

The 90% Rule is based, in part, on my years with Merrill Lynch, Waddell & Reed, Florida Professional Services Group and the Carter & Associates Law Firm. It also is based upon my personal experience of being head over heels in debt and how I got out. More importantly, this book was developed through divine inspiration from God to set all people free from the bondage of debt. God has called me to preach and to teach this ministry of prosperity throughout the four corners of the world. For such a time as this, God has called me to speak to **you** about His love for **you** and His blessings for **your** finances!

As I travel from place to place explaining **The 90% Rule**, I find that people who have applied it to their lives are utterly amazed at how simple it is to get out of debt. God would not have made it complicated. If so, only a select few could have benefited – **The 90% Rule** works for anyone and everyone. God is no respecter of persons. God wants us all to be free. This is not something I heard or read; I have lived **The 90% Rule**.

I had sunk deep into financial sin, far from the peaceful, prosperous shore, so deep in debt and stained within, sinking to rise no more. After five years of using **The 90% Rule**, see how God has blessed me. Yes, the Master of the Sea (God) heard my despairing cry from the waters of financial bondage. He lifted me, now safe and prosperous am I! **The 90% Rule** is a simple plan of how God's love will lift you from the depths of bankruptcy and despair and place you on the solid ground of financial freedom. **The 90% Rule** is my testimony from poverty to prosperity. It is a situational chronicle of my financial life and ministry to be a blessing to others. It is also a way for you to know that what God did for me He also will do for you.

The 90% Rule is a spiritual way to live on 90% of your earnings. You should pay 10%, which is your reasonable service, to God's church. Of the remaining 90%, you should pay 10% to yourself, in the form of savings. The remaining 80% should be used to pay current expenses, household operations and offerings to your church and/or ministries.

The 90% Rule is divided into two parts for your ease of understanding. In Part I: HOW TO GET OUT OF DEBT, I offer an inspirational financial management system by way of personal experience. In Part II: HOW TO OBTAIN WEALTH AND PROSPERITY, I provide spiritual and practical examples for wealth accumulation and rules to live by.

Remember these four steps:

- **Pray over your debts;**
- **Pray over your debt relief plan;**
- **Pray for financial discipline; and**
- **Pray for deliverance into wealth and prosperity**.

God will deliver you from the bondage of debt. May God bless you!

PART I:
HOW TO GET OUT OF DEBT!

Affirmation for Wealth

I am in a wealthy place!
I pray over my personal financial plan daily.
I never co-sign loans for others.
I live on a "cash-only" basis.
In the name of Jesus Christ, I will never be broke another day in my life.
I am anointed with the wealth favor of God-NOW!

Chapter One

WHY I WROTE THIS BOOK AND WHY YOU NEED IT!

Child of God, it really is important for you that you get out of debt and prosper such that the Word of God may be preached to the four corners of the world. Why did I write this book? I wrote this book because there are so many people afraid and suffering. It is written for anyone who has ever experienced loneliness, grief, heartache, physical and mental pain, poverty, homelessness, frustration and self-doubt. Additionally, it is written for anyone who has ever reached out to be more than they are, who has hoped to see more of life, who has ever wanted spiritual happiness and who wants to achieve self-actualization.

The 90% Rule is a textbook for tithers.

Why do you need this book? You need the information contained in this book to live free from worry and poverty. I also want to let you in on a little secret: When you're broke, you can't do anything! Being broke gave me a spirit of poverty and that spirit of

I wrote this book because there are so many people afraid and suffering. It is written for anyone who has ever experienced loneliness, grief, heartache, physical and mental pain, poverty, homelessness, frustration and self-doubt. You need the information contained in this book to live free from worry and poverty.

poverty in my mind gave a foothold to the devil. I couldn't think right, I didn't act right and I fell into a state of despair. From that despair, I fell into self-destructive behavior. Without the necessary finances to care for my family and meet my financial obligations, debt impacted every aspect of my life. It was painful, as depression and darkness followed me daily.

I had to write this book because God commanded it. **The 90% Rule** is a textbook for tithers. I also had to write this book because I don't want anyone, least of all Christian believers, to go through what I suffered due to a lack of finances.

In **The 90% Rule**, I want to give you all that I am through God calling me into His ministry, all that I have experienced in poverty and prosperity and all that I have learned (through reading God's Word and the words of others) to help you become more than a conqueror through Jesus Christ in your finances. So, if I'm too wordy, take what you need and leave the rest for someone else. I have written **The 90% Rule** out of the overflow of God's wisdom to me for all believers!

Life can be a series of constant surprises unless you're ready for it! Some have said how we respond to these surprises is a test of character. The American Heritage Dictionary defines character as "the combination of qualities or features that distinguishes one person, group or thing from another." Character is built through overcoming adversity – anything worthwhile, tangible or intangible requires work to attain. It will take character, on your part, to fully activate and appreciate **The 90% Rule**. A part of character also is recognizing the circumstances surrounding your life. Character is also the most important issue in the most important campaign, life.

The character of God is freedom. God wants each of us to be free from financial bondage. He has not given us a spirit of fear; he has given us a spirit of hope through our faith in Him (Romans 8:15). As such, God has promised to meet each and every one of our needs – if we seek Him first (Matthew 6:33). Christians and non-Christians have fallen prey to the Ostrich-Head-in-the-Sand mentality that says"ignore a problem long enough and it will go away." Nothing could be farther from the truth.

Who Am I?

Immediately prior to law school, I enjoyed life as a stockbroker with Merrill Lynch. I made good money, drove a Mercedes-Benz and had a ton of credit cards. In fact, I had saved a nice little nest egg for law school tuition. However, once I resigned my job at Merrill Lynch, a funny thing happened. Years earlier I had co-signed (guaranteed) a loan for a former business partner and he defaulted on the payments.

The bank, also the landlord for Merrill Lynch, served me notice of the default at my desk, as I was preparing to move out. My spouse did not hesitate to remind me that she had told me years ago that my ex-partner was a liar and a thief. Of course, she did not spare my feelings when highlighting her opinion of the quality of my judgment in the selection of friends, associates and business partners.

After some legal wrangling and much pain, hurt and domestic (husband-wife) consternation, the bank settled for me making payment. Unfortunately, this amount was my total savings from my tenure at Merrill Lynch. Therefore, I started law school broke. I also learned a very expensive lesson: **Never co-sign a loan for anyone!** Solomon warns us not to serve as "*surety for thy friend*" and I should have listened (Proverbs 6:1-2). He gives this warning because "*the wicked borroweth, and payeth not again…*" (Psalm 37:21). Child of God, I don't care if it's your family or close personal friend, please do not co-sign a loan. Regardless of the circumstances, when you borrow money you become the "*servant to the lender*" (Proverbs 22:7).

This experience was painful, humiliating and financially draining for me. Being a Christian, I left vengeance for my ex-partner to the Lord and I believed that He would make a way for me somehow. Instead of my original plan of attending law school (debt-free) on my savings, now I needed another way to finance my education. Of course, I felt a little better knowing I had my credit cards. I also applied for several loans to pay my law school tuition. I had four loans granted for three years of law school. Additionally, I used my credit cards to fill in the gaps. Those gaps became my financial Grand Canyon. It took me twelve years to pay off my student loans for law school.

The Paper Chase

Law school was a tremendous experience – the paper chase, study groups and grades on the curve system – yielding intellectual and emotional peaks and valleys. We were told, during the first day of classes, that we are the best and brightest in the country. We were being prepared to preserve democracy through the rule of law. More importantly, we would either sink or swim on our own merits. Therefore, each of us perfected the art of winning at all costs. During law school, I was selected for the Moot Court Team, competing in state and national mock trial events. Like most of my classmates, I knew I would make a lot of money after graduation.

Six months after graduation from law school, I opened my own law firm, hiring two associates. We had a great beginning – first-class office building, quality clientele – and each of us benefited greatly. In addition to an individual income, we all had dream vacations – the Caribbean and Hawaii.

The Cost Of Living

I was living the good life. There was nothing but (financial) blue skies in my future. I had a veritable cornucopia of credit cards: 10 VISAs; 8 MASTERCARDs; 2 AMERICAN EXPRESSes and numerous others. I also had rental and other investment property, a killer wardrobe and a wife and two daughters who literally shopped until they dropped. Additionally, my children attended the most exclusive (and expensive) private school in the area. Although I earned ample resources to pay off all of my bills, I chose not to. Other People's Money was the theme of the 1980s and I participated fully in this practice.

I really enjoyed living on the edge and I did not worry about anything. Actually, I was quite proud of my accomplishments and life was great. Oh yes, I had long been a Christian, accepting the Lord Jesus and baptized at twelve years old. I was richly blessed and I knew it. I paid my tithes, volunteered my time and provided free legal services to my church and knew that God would continually bless me.

I had always dreamed of going to Hawaii. Not only did I go to Hawaii, but my hotel was right on Waikiki Beach. I ate at the finest restaurants, sailed, visited local sites and went to a luau – living the life. I thought I had gone to heaven without having to die. On the seventh and final day there, an amazing thing happened to me. I was walking on the beach at six o'clock in the morning, hand-in-hand with my wife, feeling the calming breeze and playing tag with the waves of the Pacific Ocean when I stopped.

The Call

I stopped because I heard a roaring force – it was not thunder, it was a beautiful day – cataclysmically suspending me in time and space. It was a natural sound but not one ever made by man or animal. It was the voice

> **I stopped because I heard a roaring force – it was not the thunder, it was a beautiful day – cataclysmically suspending me in time and space. It was a natural sound but not one ever made by man or animal. It was the voice of God.**

of God. I could actually see – in my mind – the awesome power of the universe and He was speaking to me. "Teach the people, teach the people my word." I said yes. My wife, although closer to me than my shadow, never heard a word nor saw anything. It was God Almighty calling me and giving me my ministry, to teach the people. Teach them about freedom from financial bondage.

The most amazing thing I discovered about God's calling was that the information needed to formalize **The 90% Rule** was readily available to me. The thing I did not realize was how painful the proving process would be for me. I literally went through "the Job Experience" – from 1985 through 1997 – before finalizing **The 90% Rule** into a coherent message.

> **I assured her that I had no intentions of ever preaching, and I did not. This was because most of the preachers I knew were broke.**

I shared this

information about my calling with my wife, who reminded me that she did not want to be married to a preacher. Of course, she had told me this before we were married – since my father was a minister. I assured her that I had no intentions of ever preaching, and I did not. This was because most of the preachers I knew were broke. My father was a great preacher and a committed Christian. He accepted the call to preach when he was 20 and never retired. He died at age 79 and broke. In fact, all those churches he pastored over the years did not give us one dime. I had to borrow money to pay for his funeral. He never even owned his own home.

Good News, Bad News

Now that I had been called to preach, I thought every day would be like a holiday for me. A funny thing happened as I began to expand my law practice – to make more money. It was one of those good news, bad news situations. The good news – I was able to recruit from the *crème de la crème* (top 10%, law review, moot court national champions) of law school graduates. I awarded a new Porsche and a luxury townhouse as a signing bonus to one of my new associates and guaranteed full partner within a year. Both were guaranteed production bonuses.

Additionally, I received major contracts from a city government and a state agency. The bad news – one of my associates failed the first attempt of the bar examination and the other was not allowed to sit for the Florida Bar because he had attended an out-of-state law school. Then, my biggest client (a city government) stiffed me for a $600,000 fee. It seemed as though as soon as I accepted the call into ministry the bottom fell out for me!

My business became extremely tenuous – a doubling of work required by the remaining clients and over-extension of all of my bank loans. Speaking of my bank loans, all were signature loans (lines of credit). In my business plan, I had requested a $100,000 loan. Upon interviews with various banks, they recommended that I reduce my loan request by one half. Eventually, one bank loaned me $10,000. Later, this amount increased to $20,000 and another bank gave me a $10,000 loan. I spent nearly every waking hour working to make ends meet.

Due to these emerging circumstances, I put every dime earned back into the firm and used the balances on my credit cards for operational (day-to-day) expenses. Exactly one year into my practice I was sunk in a sea of debt. I worked to pay my employees and business overhead, yet nothing for me.

My Personal Debts in 1990

Creditor	Account Balance	Payment Amount
Gayfers	$ 239.00	$50.00
Montgomery Ward	2,400.00	115.00
First Florida Bank	20,000.00	450.87
Sun Bank (1)	10,000.00	400.00
N. Florida Credit Union	4,900.00	132.50
Blazer Financial	3,390.00	160.00
ITT Financial	397.00	50.00
Anchor Mortgage	49,500.00	535.00
GMAC	29,325.00	610.50
Manufacturers Hanover	20,000.00	730.00
Allstate	854.00	71.17
J C Penney	186.00	20.00
R & B Supply	299.00	24.92
Rumger Insurance	438.00	36.50
Sun Bank (2)	2,067.00	160.00
First National Bank	11,979.00	330.00
Sallie Mae	12,425.00	157.00
Barnett VISA	1,400.00	116.67
Sears	753.00	62.75
Discover	2,207.00	75.00
Employee Wages	2,687.00	75.00
NFECU VISA	556.00	46.33
NFECU MASTERCARD	800.00	66.67
First Bank Card (VISA/MASTERCARD)	2,353.00	150.00
LOWE's	754.00	62.83
Citibank MASTERCARD	2,254.00	118.00
Computer Tutors	2,050.00	170.83
Citibank VISA	2,312.00	87.50
Personal Loans (1) childhood friend	5,000.00	416.67
Personal Loans (2) cousin	500.00	41.67
Personal Loans (3) daughters' trust fund	1,000.00	83.33
Personal Loans (4) wife's friend	250.00	20.83
Personal Loan (5) former secretary	500.00	41.67
VISA (A)	2,000.00	166.67
VISA (B)	2,000.00	166.67
MASTERCARD (A)	2,000.00	166.67
Marine Midland Bank	61,071.00	787.50
TOTAL AMOUNT OWED:	**$260,846.00**	**$6,956.72**

NOTE: The American Express cards were not listed since they were paid in full monthly. My office rent ($500) is also not included, since I was in a month-to-month lease.

In the midst of all of this debt, my law practice collapsed. Since my associates failed to meet the credentialing requirements, I was personally overwhelmed -- bringing in and performing all the legal work. My anxiety levels rose precipitously and stress was my constant companion. I was determined not to let the quality of my work suffer. My physician admonished me to reduce my stress immediately or suffer the consequences. The physical consequences were immediate – temporary blindness. I closed my practice and took a job in state government – my income was cut in half, yet my bills remained the same.

I became acutely aware of my own mortality. I began to question the foundation of my faith such that my soul cried out like the children of Israel when they said:

I asked God: How LORD can I win souls for you and support the building of your kingdom without adequate resources? (I had been faithful, a tither, rendering service to the church and the poor, yet my life was in shambles, sick, broke, in debt, confused and upset.)

"*How can we sing the Lord's song in a strange land?*" (Psalm 137:4). I was now in unfamiliar territory. I asked God: How LORD can I win souls for you and support the building of your kingdom without adequate resources? (I had been faithful, a tither, rendering service to the church and the poor, yet my life was in shambles, sick, broke, in debt, confused and upset.)

I found myself in the uncharted waters of uncertainty and my hopes crashed upon the rocks of despair such that I literally cried out like Jesus on the cross: "*My God, my God, why hast thou forsaken me?*" (Matthew

27:46). I lost it all – my business, prestige, money and friends. Eighteen months later, I lost my family through divorce: an expensive divorce (add $75,000 to the $260,846 debt) that caused an avalanche of financial disarray from which I didn't think I'd ever recover.

Looking For Jesus

Then I began to seek Jesus through more prayer, more meditation and more giving. I gave more of my time, talents and treasure to the church. It seemed crazy to me that I could be a Christian, tither, minister and a good person, yet I was suffering. I began to wonder why bad things happen to good people. I began to meditate day and night. I started to pray all through the day about everything.

I found a job working as a temporary employee for state government. I received a promotion in my job (to full time) that was truly a mixed blessing. I was happy to earn more money, yet I was unhappy at spending less time in church. Sometimes, during the middle of the day, I would drive over to the sanctuary (in peaceful solitude) and talk to God and the prophets. The job that I took caused me to revisit the issue of predestination.

Predestination is defined as "the act whereby God is believed to have foreordained all things." In essence, we are mere pawns and there is nothing we can do to change our lot in life. You can fall so deep into debt that you will believe anything just to maintain. In my case, although I was earning more, all I did with my income was make minimum payments on my bills. There were too many to pay off. My new job required me to serve as director of a division of state government with 127 employees, where morale was at an all-time low. I thought, wow, how could God put me in this situation when I was suffering. I had to forget my troubles and concerns to lift the spirits of all these people.

The head of the agency, that hired me, said I was a natural for this job. If he only had known about the economic chaos in my life, he probably would have hired someone else. The major external issue facing the division was a billion dollar corporation (which we regulated) that was going bankrupt and taking $400 million of the taxpayers' money with them. By the grace of God through much prayer, hard work and tenacious negotiations, we were able to resolve the bankruptcy. A lot of my Merrill Lynch and legal experience came in handy, but prayer got me through this. Through prayer, teamwork and listening, my employees began to feel good about themselves and their jobs. We had enthusiasm and efficiency at an all-time high. My boss told me that I had done a great job!

From Grandma To Greatness

William Shakespeare said, "Be not afraid of greatness; some men are born great, some achieve greatness and some have greatness thrust upon them." What about you? Are you content with watching things happen to you, or would you rather make things happen for you? In the context of predestination, I always have believed that rarely during a millennium does opportunity coincide with destiny for a person. I have known since age twelve that I was born to greatness, which I define as service for God. I also have known that one day opportunity and destiny would come together in my life – God would anoint me into ministry with a mission. **The 90% Rule** is my ministry with a mission for the entire world.

At twelve years old, I had a debilitating illness (severe asthma and pneumonia) and was given only two weeks to live. After receiving this terminal diagnosis, my mother took me home to my grandma. Grandma was a praying woman who believed God could do anything but fail. I answered yes to the following three questions my grandmother asked, which allowed me to never look back. **Do you believe that Jesus Christ is the Son of God? Do you believe that Jesus Christ died for the remission (forgiveness) of your sins? Do you believe that Jesus Christ is your Lord and Savior, who will deliver you from all hurt and harm?**

Now I know what the Apostle Paul meant, when he said: "*And we know that all things work together for good to them that love God, to them who are the called according to his purpose*" (Romans 8:28). God healed me from my deadly illness for a heavenly purpose.

In essence, why must it be Matthew Carter who takes the message of Holy prosperity throughout the four corners of the world? Since the Spirit of God has come upon me to preach his Gospel, the anointing of the Holy Spirit requires me *to preach good tidings to the meek.* (Luke 4:18) The first mission of a minister of the Gospel is to share the good news with those most in need. Freedom from economic bondage is indeed good news. There is no better teaching to a poor person than how to receive prosperity. **The 90% Rule** is a ministry that will benefit people worldwide. God has called me to teach the people the Spiritual Method for debt free living. This is my destiny. This is my calling. This is my purpose in ministry.

Why Me?

Why was I chosen by God to teach you about achieving freedom from debt? Jesus when he called Simon Peter to his ministry told him that "*Satan hath desired you . . . But I have prayed for thee . . . and when thou are converted, strengthen thy brethren*" (Luke 22:31-32). The Lord blessed me with more than 20 years of experience with managing financial resources for businesses and individuals. He also gave me a love for teaching and a spiritual gift for the same. Like thousands of Americans my life has been racked with setbacks and sorrows. I have plenty of battle scars and a great testimony!

When Jesus called me to preach his Gospel, he had to reach W-A-Y down for me. He told me there are millions of people like me, and I can bring my experience with His grace to their assistance. Because of my calling into ministry, years of financial counseling experience and my testimony, now I can truly strengthen the brethren (all believers).

My wife and I met when I was 17 and in high school. We were both Baptist, which was no small thing to my grandma, who loved her dearly. In fact, my grandma chose her as my wife. We dated for five years before marriage. As husband and wife, we survived a lot of situations and circumstances: we survived illiteracy (both college-educated, she has Ph.D. and I have a law degree), we survived poverty (earning more in a year than our parents did most of their working lives), we survived distance (my being in the Army for more than three years – stateside and in Germany – and her away at school in different states), we survived family tragedy (a child born with a birth defect) and we survived my call into ministry.

However, we didn't survive our loss of income and financial stability. To put it in the vernacular, "romance without finance is a nuisance." After eighteen years of wedded bliss, because financial shortcomings magnified every little concern into a major problem, we were divorced.

It seemed that for a two-year period nothing went right in life for me. Despite what was happening around me, I seemed to be my own worst enemy. I had fallen into sins of co-mission, omission and disposition. I knew God was there, I just thought I could handle things better myself. Two years after our divorce, I met, married and divorced my second wife. The entire experience lasted about sixteen months. Although we never completed the premarital counseling course, we decided to get married anyway. We had a big beautiful expensive wedding, but underneath I had only internal turmoil. Thinking of this 16-month experience, I know what James meant when he said, "*a double-minded man is unstable in all his ways*" (James 1:8).

Because of myriad issues, all stemming from a lack of finances, I had become double-minded. I was praying to God but counting on my personal abilities to resolve my problems. I was looking for love in all the wrong places. I was allowing depression, frustration and guilt to so overwhelm me it clouded my judgment. My clouded judgment caused me to emotionally hurt others close to me.

The debt from this divorce was now layered on top of my earlier divorce and debt. Consequently, one year later, I filed for bankruptcy. I thought I had lost it all earlier, but now I knew I had lost everything – because I had lost even hope. The worst day in my life was waking up one morning to take my youngest daughter to visit my sister and my car had been repossessed the night before as we slept. I had made a payment arrangement with the bank and sent in the funds. They still repossessed my car. I learned a lot about creditors and how they say one thing and do another when you're behind in your payments.

I was at the end of my rope – I felt like a failure in love, a failure in finances and a failure in life. Although I did not cry at my mother's funeral at age 15, I literally sobbed buckets of tears. I cannot describe the pain I felt when my daughter looked up at me and asked what happened to our car. This is the most humiliating experience I have ever had in my life. I was at the end of my rope and all I knew how to do, at this point in time, was call on God.

When I found myself thinking the unthinkable, something deep inside me would not let me give up. I could tell that God never gave up on me. He did not withdraw His calling from my life. Notwithstanding all of the turmoil and feelings of inadequacy, I knew I could never give up on God. I knew this because God never gave up on me. I continued to pray, continued to preach (although my opportunities were greatly diminished) and I continued to follow God's mission for my life – teach His people how to get out of debt and prosper. **The 90% Rule** was blessed by God and empowered through the Holy Spirit for all the people of the world. It is God's practical message to the multitudes.

The inspiration of the Holy Spirit has ordained **The 90% Rule** to assist you during these troubled and changing economic times. God is a right now God. He is always ready to help in any facet of our lives during the times we need Him most. I am living proof. It does not matter what a person's nationality is, poverty and fear do not discriminate. As humans we do not know what the future holds for us and some may desperately fear the future.

I don't know what the future holds, but I do know who holds the future. God holds our future because He's always there for us "*from everlasting to everlasting, thou art God*" (Psalms 90:2). **The 90% Rule** allows us to be as David when he overcame his fear. "*I sought the LORD, and he heard me, and delivered me from all my fears*" (Psalms 34:4). **The 90% Rule** is your economic freedom through the blessing of Almighty God. **Believers from around the World, let us go forward together in prosperity!**

Affirmation for Wealth

I am in a wealthy place!
I do not look back.
I fight the good fight of faith daily.
I am more than a conqueror through Christ Jesus.
In the name of Jesus Christ, I will never be broke another day in my life.
I am anointed with the wealth favor of God-NOW!

Chapter Two

IN THE BEGINNING

I was broke and all of my bills were at least two months overdue. I felt overwhelmed by my financial obligations. I had borrowed all the money – from banks, friends and family – that I could, trying to keep my law practice going. In addition, I did not want to lessen my standard of living. It was extremely stressful and I was not making progress. I was like a number of other people, worried about the tremendous financial problems in my life. In short, I could not sleep or concentrate clearly because I was in bondage to debt.

I was like a number of other people, worried about the tremendous financial problems in my life. In short, I could not sleep or concentrate clearly because I was in bondage to debt.

It would be wonderful to live free from worry. After all, we are beset by the vicissitudes of life and the demands of living in a free enterprise society. Everything costs – time, money, food, shelter, etc. – and it seems that we need everything in order to make it. My financial situation was not unlike a number of other people's. Everyday I pick up my newspaper or turn on the television or radio news, I discover hundreds of thousands of Americans and millions from around the world losing their jobs and homes. Additionally, I see millions of refugees from the war-torn and politically unstable areas of the world on their way to America. A sampling of their reasons for wanting to come to America revealed one common thread: America is the land of great economic opportunity.

I saw everything and everyone else as the cause of my problems. I was doing everything right and honorable, so bad things should not happen to me. I screamed out to God and asked again: "Why do bad things happen to good people?" The tight-fisted banks would loan me only enough money to guarantee failure. The only contract legal work available from the government required law firms to have a minimum of three or more attorneys. By now I was only a solo practitioner, meaning it was only me to do it all. It also meant that there would be no government contracts.

The clients I had preferred to pay their other obligations rather than their (my) legal fees. It was amazing to me that they would choose to ignore that I had family obligations as well. Amazingly, many of them were churches. Almost all were members of churches – Christians. I understood that they had other responsibilities, and consequently I reduced my fees. Yet I still did not get paid. Rather than taking these lemons and making lemonade, I became bitter.

I lost it all and I was mad – mad at my debts, mad at my debtors and mad at God.

I could not believe this was happening to me. This was not the way I planned it. I had done well in law school, and I was providing quality legal services in my law practice. I could not understand why people were not flocking to my office. More importantly, I could not understand why people were not paying for my services. The Word of God tells me not to sue a Christian and I did not. It seemed hard to adhere to the Word of God when, all around me, fellow Christians were shirking their legal obligations to pay for services rendered. In view of the fact that I was also providing free legal services to my church and several other community organizations, it hurt even more. Surely these God fearing Christians had read: "*For the scripture saith, Thou shalt not muzzle the ox that treadeth out the corn. And, the laborer is worthy of his reward*" (1 Timothy 5:18). They had benefited from my services – some of them were able to keep their homes, maintain their businesses and avoid prosecution – yet they were unwilling to pay.

I was tithing, attending all church services (worship, Bible study, prayer meeting, training, etc.) and had a daily prayer life at home. Things, however, were no better -- mounting debts, slow pay and no-pay clients. I was like the woman with the issue of blood – spent all, searched everywhere for relief and still no better (Mark 5:25-24). I lost it all and I was mad – mad at my debts, mad at my debtors and mad at God. The frustration of poverty is not a good feeling. Being broke makes you stupid. It was really stupid for me to get mad with God. He was the only one who could help me and the only one who loved me. Stupid people make stupid mistakes – over and over – I did with my finances and my family.

Before The Fall

By all indications, I was doing very well financially. I was making upwards of $80,000.00 in net income. Prior to my first divorce, my wife was earning over $30,000 and we were looked upon as a middle-class family. Our two daughters were in private school, costing $8,000 yearly for tuition. On paper, we looked financially well off, but in reality we were one paycheck away from disaster. Like a lot of people, including well-meaning Christians, I thought my high income would continue, my health would never fail and I would never have to care about bills. Unfortunately, just when I thought things were at their best – the bottom fell out!

The Fall

First, I lost the largest client for my law practice (remember that $600,000 city?). We obtained a larger financial settlement (for them) than they anticipated, yet they refused to pay us the agreed-upon higher fee. We had represented them on a contingency fee, yet when the money came in they thought the amount we were to receive was too high. The press and their constituents seized upon the issue of our fee and ignored that we brought them more than $6,000,000 in income. We eventually settled for less than we had honestly earned.

Secondly, I had to let one of my lawyers go and the other one quit. I had to give up my legal secretary. My landlord sold the office building and the new owner would not renew my lease. I had to give up a major contract because it required a law firm with at least three attorneys, and all I had left was myself.

Finally, all the banks called in my signature loans at the same time. My attitude for success crashed upon the hard rocks of reality – professional financial disaster. I could not believe this was happening to me. I had wanted to be a lawyer since I was four years old and I had finally made it. I did well in law school and started my practice six months after graduation. How could this happen to me? Nine months after opening the doors to my, seemingly successful, law practice, I had to close them.

During the fall of 1989, I accepted the call to pul service. To be more accurate, I beat a path to the door ol state government and begged for a job. Initially, I was hired as a temporary employee to provide research and assistance. Later, I began (full time) as a bureau chief. I was then promoted to Division Director. My salary went from $40,000 to $62,000 annually.

The prelude to my appointment was the billion-dollar bankruptcy of a major development company. It was the largest land developer in Florida, having planned and built several cities. The State of Florida had accepted $400,000,000 worth of worthless development bonds from General Development Company.

In my new position, I worked very hard (sometimes 20 hours a day) to ensure that the taxpayers of Florida were not stuck with a $400,000,000 boondoggle. "60 Minutes" did a story on this fiasco and it was the daily fare of the major newspapers in Florida. More importantly, I felt the more than 100,000 people around the world who had purchased home sites in Florida deserved fairness.

I remembered the golden rule and put myself in the place of those who had bought home sites. Working through the courts, with a team of lawyers, bankers, accountants and developers, we came up with a land exchange program. The exchange program guaranteed a home site to those purchasers who were not in default and provided real estate to guarantee the creditworthiness of the bond issue.

Exactly one month after the court order approving the exchange program, I was asked to resign. After my new boss had praised my efforts in resolving this problem, I was rewarded by a forced resignation. My attitude again became bitter. It was unfathomable to me that after the cost savings to the taxpayers and protection for home site purchasers, I was asked to leave. I had always believed that an employee who did an outstanding job would be rewarded, rather than fired. Where was "60 Minutes" now? Where were the reporters and satisfied homebuyers, bankers, investors and citizens of Florida, now that I needed them? More importantly, after the fall I had a question: **Where was God?**

Affirmation for Wealth

I am in a wealthy place!

I call those things that are not as though they were.

I know in my heart that I have been blessed with wealth and prosperity.

In the name of Jesus Christ, I will never be broke another day in my life.

I am anointed with the wealth favor of God- NOW!

Chapter Three

A QUESTION FOR GOD

I asked God, how could this happen to me? I had worked hard, kept my nose clean and by any objective measure had done a great job, yet I was forced to resign. I had the attitude of frustration (from the failure of my law practice), betrayal (from a dishonorable employer) and fear (maybe God had forgotten me).

This problem of being overwhelmed is nowhere more predominant than in the economic lives of Christians and non-Christians in America.

Christians are not supposed to look at the onslaught of the world's problems and cry, Why me? Christians are supposed to remember the life of Jesus and say, Why not me? It's easy to say now, but at the time I was too consumed with my problems to think spiritually. This problem of being overwhelmed is nowhere more predominant than in the economic lives of Christians and non-Christians in America. America is no longer an isolated place. The world is at our doorsteps. Economists have dubbed the world as a global community.

With minimum income and maximum expenses, disaster was just around the corner.

In this global community, how did we, Christians and nonbelievers, get into such a financial quagmire? The Apostle Paul reminds us that "*. . . for whatsoever a man soweth, that shall he also reap*" (Galatians 6:7). All of that living on credit finally caught up with me like the millions of others who had the buy-now-pay-later mentality. All of that relying on an employer for my substance and ignoring God had finally caught up with us. During the growth and good times of the 1980s, a large number of us lived on credit. Now it was time for us to pay. The 1990s required discipline to deal with unemployment, recession and economic stagnation, which I didn't have. With minimum income and maximum expenses, disaster was just around the corner. Your attitude determines your altitude and mine had hit rock bottom.

"If charge-it was the catch phrase for the 1980s, then bankruptcy became the by-word for the 1990s," stated Fred A. Schneyer, in his article in the *Tallahassee Democrat* entitled: "Bankruptcy Explosion – More people are choosing it as a way out of financial chaos." For example, in the Federal Court District of North Florida (where I live), bankruptcy filings went from a low in 1980 of 115 to a high of 653 in 1991. In 1998, more than a million people in the United States had filed for bankruptcy. By 2000, the number exceeded one and one half million. I am a living example and a contributor to these statistics.

The 90% Rule is a Spirit-filled way that anyone (male, female, black, white, brown, yellow, etc.) can become debt free. No education, experience or special skills are required for your success from The 90% Rule.

An Unkept Commitment

I made a personal commitment to never file for bankruptcy. I felt that my honor was on the line and I would dishonor God if I filed for bankruptcy. When I prayed to God for financial relief, he did not give me money. He gave me **The 90% Rule**. There's an old proverb that says, "feed a man fish, you feed him for a day, but teach a man to fish, you feed him for life." Money would have fed me for only a day (short time) but the ministry with a mission of **The 90% Rule** is feeding me for life. The Lord gave me all I needed to succeed but I was too busy feeling let down to focus on it. When God called me, he armed me with this knowledge yet I did not fully appreciate this gift of ministry until my finances collapsed.

The collapse was not because I could not pay my bills; it was because I did not that caused my financial ruin. When I was making a high income was the time for me to pay off my bills. Yet the more I made, the more I spent.

I should have listened sooner. I should have remembered to "*trust in the LORD with all* [my] *heart; and lean not unto* [my] *own understanding. In all* [my] *ways acknowledge him, and he shall direct* [my] *paths*" (Proverbs 3:5-6). I was too busy living the high life to listen to the still small voice within me. **The 90% Rule** is God's gift of ministry to me. I understand it as a way to live free from the worry of debt – in essence, doing better with the resources that God has blessed me with such that I may tell others.

The 90% Rule is a Spirit-filled way that anyone (male, female, black, white, brown, yellow, etc.) can become debt-free. No education, experience or special skills are required for your success from **The 90% Rule**, whosoever will let them come. A key for me to remember was it did not take overnight to get into this financial mess and I did not get out overnight. From 1985 to 1997, I lived financially foolish and got into a tremendous load of debt. However, from 1998 to 2002, I have reduced my total debt to less than 19% of my income by living **The 90% Rule**. Whatever time and effort it takes, I am committed to continue living **The 90% Rule**. It takes time, discipline and faith to defeat the demon of debt. I must trust in God to meet all of my needs and lean on His leadership to direct me into financial freedom.

Economic hard times are no respecter of persons. The vicious cycle of earning little and spending more has been a way of life for many people, including Christians. Many people who relied on their union to negotiate high wages and benefits now live on unemployment, food stamps and federal subsistence. To enjoy financial success I had to learn to live like Jesus. "*I must work the works of him that sent me, while it is day: the night cometh, when no man can work*" (John 9:4).

A significant number of people, once making substantial incomes, are now unemployed, without medical benefits and are part of the homeless of the nation. Many times during my ministry of **The 90% Rule**, I had ample opportunity and logical reasons to give up. I lost my job, was unemployed for more than eighteen months, went through two very expensive divorces (wherein I lost my home, car and all other assets) and then had two surgical operations within one year with no health insurance. My stress levels were so high that they almost blinded me. I felt as if there was very little left to live for.

I began to question everything, even my beliefs. I began to wonder what kind of God would allow his servant to suffer and not deliver him – when he had promised otherwise. I even questioned the foundation of my value system. Personally, I never thought bankruptcy would ever become an option for me. Unfortunately, with mounting debts and no income, it was inevitable. I reached the point of no return. In 1997, I filed for Chapter 7 protection under the bankruptcy laws. It was bad enough to be broke; now I had to be humiliated by filing for bankruptcy. All I could say, over and over, was: "My God, my God, why have thou forsaken me?"

My personal pledge not to file for bankruptcy gave way to my common sense of protecting my household. As a single parent, I knew that my children still had to eat and needed clothes and a place to live. I did not have the income to meet all of my debts. I searched high and low for jobs, even entry level, but could not find employment. After my forced resignation, I was unemployed for 18 months. Even my close Christian friends (including fellow church members), some of whom I had helped gain employment, would not give me a part-time job. Most of them wouldn't even return my phone calls.

Many people who claim to be Christians are really demons in disguise. Now I knew what it felt like to be totally alone. I had no one and I had nothing. All I could do was pray because God was the only one who would talk to me. I sought employment as an attorney, a pastor and a manager, all to no avail. I prayed about whether I should file for bankruptcy and asked God for directions. The next day, buried beneath the fold in the local newspaper, I saw that Montgomery Ward had filed for bankruptcy. Ironically, the largest amount I owed to a department store was to Montgomery Ward!

Looking for Christians, Finding God

As I went through this struggle – seeking from Christians – I found very few living Christians. Most were just talking Christians. They talked a good game but they failed to act on their words. The most shocking thing I discovered about a lot of those who profess Christianity is that they are embarrassed and uneasy talking about debt or providing assistance to those in debt. I also found out that it is very humbling to be a lawyer when the only paying job available was that as a janitor.

However, I was glad to get this job and provide for my family. In this whole process, I got closer to God and learned more about myself. I got to know Jesus, my savior and Lord. I got to know myself as a good man who would not stoop to a life of crime or addiction, but who would be thankful for the work of menial labor before I let my family suffer.

By filing for bankruptcy, I was able to hold all collections and lawsuits for collections in abeyance until the bankruptcy was final. I was able to keep the only one asset I still owned, my home. At least my daughters and I would not be homeless. We lost our telephone service and electric utilities for a time. Notwithstanding the fact that some creditors did not want to cooperate, I was able to emerge from the bankruptcy with my home. When you fall behind on your debt, you'll see the other side of your creditors and it won't be very positive. The collections personnel in most corporations, at least those with whom I dealt, are from the underbelly of society. They are rude, unethical and less than truthful. If you have not had to deal with these people, count yourself fortunate. If you're falling behind in your bills, you'll see them soon.

Those who seek bankruptcy protection these days are just as likely to be middle-income people who recently lost their jobs or had to shutter their own company. This I know from personal experience. I was middle class, earning more than $120,000 in family income—until I lost my business and lost my job. Others have been forced to flee to bankruptcy court after being hit with major hospital or medical bills they couldn't afford. After two major surgeries and no health insurance or savings, I also became a statistic. The borrowing frenzy of the 1990s placed a double whammy on families.

The Tax Reform Act of 1986 removed the deduction for all interest, except that paid for mortgages, while leaving businesses with their deductions and even improving some. This, in effect, reduced the amount and number of tax refunds received by families. Secondly, most installment and credit card debt was moved to the home mortgage. The home equity loan craze caused millions of people to move unsecured (and without the tax deduction, unproductive interest) debt onto their home mortgages. When the other shoe fell, unexpected emergencies (illness, lost jobs, divorce, etc.), there was no equity remaining and no way to make the increased mortgage payments. The net effect was hundreds of thousands of homes went unsold because of their high prices (due to numerous loans). Also, millions of Americans lost their homes, jobs, families and some even lost their lives. After all I had been through; I was ready for a change. **How about you?**

Affirmation for Wealth

I am in a wealthy place!
Whatever God did for Abraham, He will do for me because of His promise.
In the name of Jesus Christ, I will never be broke another day in my life.
The tithe belongs to God.
The rest belongs to me.
I am anointed with the wealth favor of God-NOW!

Chapter Four

WE'RE ALL TOGETHER NOW

There were a few things I had to do to get on "the straight and narrow." I had to make up my mind that I was sick and tired of being in debt. Like I did, in order to live free from worry, you must be ready, willing and able to change your mind. You must be ready, willing and able to change your mind about how you feel and stop being overwhelmed by debts. "*The rich ruleth over the poor, and the borrower is the servant to the lender*" (Proverbs 22:7). Once you change your mind you can change your life.

The United States government outlawed racial slavery by the Thirteenth Amendment in 1865. However, the economic slavery facing us today is more insidious and far more dangerous – it affects us all, black and white, male and female, Christian and non-Christian. The economic slavery facing us today is legal and practiced worldwide. If you only earn enough to make the minimum payment on your monthly bills, you are a slave to debt. Jesus died to set us free and we have allowed credit card companies, banks, mortgage companies and myriad other creditors to enslave us on the credit plantations forever.

The United States government outlawed racial slavery by the Thirteenth Amendment in 1865. However, the economic slavery facing us today is more insidious and far more dangerous – it affects us all, black and white, male and female, Christian and non-Christian.

I thought I knew about slavery and injustice, but it was not until, by the Grace of God, I took a close look at my personal financial situation that I understood real slavery. No racial group gets preferential treatment – we all suffer. In order to stave off the creditor wolves, I had to beg, borrow and scrape every dollar possible. A few of my friends, the higher interest finance companies and some family members loaned me money. It was all too little, with too short of a repayment schedule and too late to make a dent in the outstanding principal. Like millions of other Americans, the economic bottom had fallen out for me.

The United States has a republic form of government based on the free enterprise system. For well over two hundred years, it has endured through all types of economic cycles – inflation, recession, depression, wars, natural disasters, etc. – to become the most dominant and robust economy on the planet. In fact, nearly every nation on the globe has now begun to embrace certain aspects of free enterprise to get the most production from their economies and higher standards of living for their peoples.

Understanding the free enterprise system has helped all people – the poor, uneducated, minorities, immigrants, etc. – to participate in the "American Dream" of becoming wealthy. Generally speaking, the free enterprise system allows the marketplace to drive the supply and demand for goods and services. The quantity of the supply and the quality of the demand determine the prices paid for these goods and services. It is critical that Christians learn as much as possible about the free enterprise economic system, otherwise you will fall victim to always being a consumer (buying) and never a producer (selling).

Consumers buy the goods provided by the producers. It is critical that everyone on the planet understand this economic system because the world is a global community – capitalism is everywhere. It is also critically important that we get an understanding of basic financial concepts (tithing, offering, budgeting, saving, investing, etc.) and begin to use them as soon as possible.

> **"In many respects, improving basic financial education at the elementary and secondary school level can provide a foundation for financial literacy, helping younger people avoid poor financial decisions that can take years to overcome."**
> **Alan Greenspan**

The 90% Rule will help you to fully understand how to survive in the global economy. In fact, Federal Reserve Chairman Alan Greenspan says it is critical that we improve "financial literacy" among children and adults in the United States. "In many respects, improving basic financial education at the elementary and secondary school level can provide a foundation for financial literacy, helping younger people avoid poor financial decisions that can take years to overcome," Greenspan said. He is absolutely right, particularly for Christians. How can you be a blessing to the household of faith (the church) when you have no resources to perform even your reasonable service (i.e., bring your tithes and offerings to God's house)?

The 90% Rule recognizes that children need to learn about economics earlier because they are getting into more debt earlier than ever before. "Like no other generation, today's 18- to 35- year olds have grown up with a culture of debt – a product of easy credit, a booming economy and expensive lifestyles." Stated Christine Dugas in a *USA Today* article, entitled: "Debt smothers America's youth": "They often live from paycheck to paycheck, using credit cards and loans to finance restaurant meals, high-tech toys and new cars they couldn't otherwise afford, according to market researchers, debt counselors and consumer advocates." Consequently, before they can even get into the working world, a large number of our young people are overwhelmed by debt.

This group of young people really needs **The 90% Rule** in order to break the cycle of debt and live a life of wealth and prosperity. We really need to teach, as Chairman Greenspan says, financial literacy to our children at an early age. Ms. Dugas went on to say in her article, "At a time when they could be setting aside money for a down payment on a home, many young people are mortgaging their financial future. Instead of getting a head start on saving for retirement, they are spending years digging themselves out of debt."

After twelve years of financial hell, I finally got serious with **The 90% Rule**. **The 90% Rule** helped me to overcome my years of financial illiteracy and frustration. Now that **The 90% Rule** is part of my life I will never be broke another day in my life!

Richer and Poorer

My fellow believers, you really need the wisdom of God concerning your finances otherwise you are destined to go through the fire as I did. Today the former middle class is becoming the working poor and, often times, the poor, broke and the hungry. People think they are getting ahead by charging themselves into oblivion. Yet, there are more bankruptcies and hopelessness than ever. In the meantime, the number of billionaires has risen from less than 50 in 1980 to more than 100 in 2002. In fact, a large number of the wealthiest people in the world live in the United States. Bill Gates, of Microsoft, the richest man in the world, is said to be worth more than $80 billion.

Consequently, they are killing, robbing and committing violence in record numbers – all to get money and other valuables, to support their lifestyles and terrorize hard-working decent law-abiding citizens. There are others, living in suburbia and downtown, who live for the fast easy money, obtained by any means, legal or illegal. Even some Christians are looking for an easy way out and are taking short cuts to bring in extra money.

The result of this phenomenon is a common lament by numerous inner city gang members, drug dealers and other members of the subterranean economy. "The rich gets richer and the poor gets poorer." Consequently, they have used this as a justification to turn to a life of crime. There has been an entire generation of hopeless Americans born and are now coming of age in the inner cities.

This generation believes that life is cheap and not worth living. Consequently, they are killing, robbing and committing violence in record numbers – all to get money and other valuables to support their lifestyles and terrorize hard-working decent law-abiding citizens. There are others, living in suburbia and downtown, who live for the fast easy money, obtained by any means, legal or illegal.

Even some Christians are looking for an easy way out and are taking short cuts to bring in extra money.

The results of this mentality and of people becoming "field hands" on the economic plantation have created a disturbing phenomenon. A generation of Americans entering adulthood, for the first time in 100 years, may not achieve a better lifestyle than their parents. As a child, I knew that I would live better off economically than my parents. Neither had any formal education, yet I became a lawyer. However, with the national personal debt crisis, my children may find it impossible to achieve a better lifestyle than mine. With the debt crisis of the eighties, people working more and earning less in the nineties, coupled with the cost cutting measures of government and private industry, it feels like the middle class has all but disappeared.

The goal of the world's system of economics is to get money from you to generate profits. The goal of The 90% Rule is to get money to you.

In essence, a number of people who felt financially secure five years ago are one paycheck away from poverty. Some are worse off – bankrupt and homeless. Part of the problem is self-induced and part put upon us by our misunderstanding of the free enterprise system. The goal of the world's system of economics is to get money from you to generate profits. The goal of **The 90% Rule** is to get money to you for wealth and prosperity.

The American Dream has always been to reach the middle class – home ownership, car and college for the kids, a pension – the good life. My generation, "the baby boomers," grew up believing that we would make it. Indeed, the growth of the middle class – one of the underpinnings of democracy in this country – has been reversed. Because a large number have succumbed to the slavery of debt, there has been a dismantling of the middle class.

The economic malaise facing the Christian Church and the country, as a backdrop, has caused too many people to paint an uneasy feeling of doom throughout all financial markets. Politicians, civic leaders, business executives and even church leaders have held up this catastrophic canvass as a mirror and individuals have painted a portrait of poverty for themselves and their families. Rather than using the tax policies to their benefit, most Americans are throwing up their hands in frustration and disgust.

A lost generation – poorer than their parents, the vanishing middle class, skyrocketing returns and shrinking tax rates on investments for the very wealthy are but a few of the results of the attitude of economic helplessness. More and more adult children are returning to the "empty nest," that is to say, returning to live with their parents. The cost of living, particularly home ownership, is beyond reach of a growing number of full time employed people.

Christians and non-Christians have been ridiculed and even lampooned by the leaders of business and government as lazy American workers and "Joe Lunch Bucket." However, it is this average American who keeps the economic ship of state afloat.

Joe Lunch Bucket

Christians and non-Christians have been ridiculed and even lampooned by the leaders of business and government as lazy American workers and "Joe Lunch Bucket." However, it is this average American who keeps the economic ship of state afloat. The average American, although hardworking, generally spends all he or she earns and borrows more than he or she makes. Just the cost of living (i.e., basics – food, clothing, shelter) may take all the average person earns. It is little wonder there is so much debt and people have very little disposable income. Tithing and charitable contributions are difficult for the average person to make from his or her meager earnings.

Before **The 90% Rule,** I was like the typical worker, living from paycheck to paycheck. Then, a week after payday, I was wondering where the money went. I had nothing to show for my entire pay period (sometimes bi-weekly, sometimes monthly). "Joe Lunch Bucket is a name that's given to those who live from paycheck to paycheck and are up to their ears in consumer and credit card debt," says Barbara Martin, in her book, Minimum Wage to Maximum Wealth.

In her book, Ms. Martin also talks about how some people are using shopping as a form of therapy. "When things get tough, the tough go shopping." Unfortunately, more and more people are using shopping as a type of poor folks' therapy for their depression. Shopping on credit makes a bad situation worse. I'm living proof that when you do this you feel worse. You also feel like there's no way out for you. It is a vicious cycle that, left unchecked, will destroy you mentally, physically and financially. "I've been there and done that" – it almost deprived me of my joy. I had to say, it's time to stop this madness. There should be some quality of life. The amount of energy from multiple jobs is nothing compared to the amount of time spent worrying about bills.

> **"When things get tough the tough go shopping."**
> **Barbara Martin**

We should not have to work every day only to have nothing at the end of the month, except more bills. If you think you're going to get out of a mountain of debt while continuing to spend yourself into oblivion, you're not thinking rationally. When I read the newspapers, watch and listen to news on television and radio, see people suffering nationwide, and hear the groaning of our church congregations, I know it's time for **The 90% Rule**.

We have a way out – after we've finished praying, we need to start doing. **The 90% Rule** provides a way for Christians to be "*doers of the word*" (James 1:22). Praying will help you spiritually and mentally to practice the biblical method for reducing debt and building wealth.

Why, Lord, I keep asking myself, do your people (Christians) suffer financially? I know why I had problems -- spending more than I made and never paying off an entire balance – but why do others suffer? My answer and my confirmation (that God wanted me to write **The 90% Rule**) came from the late Rev. David Henderson. Rev. Henderson was Pastor of the Jacob Chapel Freewill Baptist Church in Tallahassee, Florida. For two and a half years, I served as his Director of Christian Education. He constantly reminded us that we should get back to the basics of living. He described the basics of living as to pray, listen and obey God.

We are no longer Joe Lunch Buckets; we are children of God. He called us a holy, peculiar people, a royal priesthood (Ephesians 1:4; Titus 2:14; 1 Peter 2:5).

I had been researching, reading, preaching, teaching and praying about **The 90% Rule** for over ten years. Dr. Henderson reminded me of Solomon when he prayed to God after building the Temple. After Solomon built the Lord's temple, he dedicated it with a praise service by all of Israel. Then God answered:

"I have heard thy prayer, and have chosen this place to myself for a house of sacrifice. If I shut up heaven that there be no rain, or if I command the locusts to devour the land, or if I send pestilence among my people; If my people, which are called by my name, shall humble themselves, and pray, and seek my face, and turn from their wicked ways; then will I hear from heaven, and will forgive their sin, and will heal their land" (II Chronicles 7:12-14).

If we are Christians, then we are God's people and we are called by his name. We are no longer "Joe Lunch Buckets"; we are children of God. He called us *a holy, peculiar people, a royal priesthood* (Ephesians 1:4; Titus 2:14; 1 Peter 2:5). Really, as Christians, we should be looked upon as morally upstanding, prosperous, decent, fair-minded and loving people.

This is what the people of God should look like. Then we should humble ourselves to God and let God be God in our lives. God is the *author and finisher of our faith* and He has all power in heaven and earth (Hebrews 12:2). We turn from our wicked ways by stopping the madness of spending and borrowing more than we can afford. It is madness to spend our families into oblivion on borrowed money. A Christian knows that the borrower is the servant to the lender. However, we are to serve only God. **The 90% Rule** is God's way of healing our (financial) land.

One of the most fundamental reasons I believe God told me to teach **The 90% Rule** is that every believer deserves dignity and decency. It is not God's wish that *any* of us *should perish.* He wants us to have the desires of our hearts (II Peter 3:9). We need to practice the Word of God in our words, actions and thoughts and He will bless us – in our hearts. He will bless us in our relationships. He will bless us in our finances. He will bless us in our bodies. He will bless us in our living and giving. He sent his only son, Jesus, to save us. All we have to do is believe (John 3:16). Jesus, himself, came that we may have a more abundant life. (John 10:10.) In essence, he came to guarantee our prosperity. **We must get our minds and attitudes focused on the quest for righteousness through faith and God will richly bless us.**

Affirmation for Wealth

I am in a wealthy place!
I treat every dollar I earn as if it belongs to God.
Before I make any purchase I will ask myself:
Do I need it?
Do I want it?
Can I do without it?
In the name of Jesus Christ, I will never be broke another day in my life.
I am anointed with the wealth favor of God-NOW!

Chapter Five

ALL ABOARD!

God had been preparing me all this time and I didn't even know it. I was too worried about my problems and hurt by my circumstances to recognize God's truth. Once I submitted to Jesus Christ both as Lord and Savior, I understood the scope of my calling. I had limited Jesus to the role of Savior only, whereas He wants to be both Lord

I had limited Jesus to the role of Savior only, whereas He wants to be both Lord and Savior. Once I did so, the Lord blessed me with finances, health, purpose and family reconciliation.

and Savior. Once I did so, the Lord blessed me with finances, health, purpose and family reconciliation. Most importantly, now I know that I must depend on Jesus Christ for everything and He will direct and protect all aspects of my life.

Your attitude does indeed determine your altitude. If you let your mind become infatuated with commercials, you will spend all that you make, beg, borrow or steal just to buy illusions. **The 90% Rule** is our way to apply common sense to our name brand spending and morality to our financial being. It provides the full economic armor of God that protects us from the fiery darts of the demons of debt (Ephesians 6:11-18). When you get the basic understanding of the free enterprise system, you will understand the significance of television, radio, magazine, newspaper and billboard advertising—to get you to buy. This is also the sole reason that we have malls, shopping centers, stores and service stations.

Once I stopped feeling sorry for myself long enough to pray and ask God what His mission was for my life, I got the right attitude. Once I stopped being angry with God and the world, I could listen to His voice. When I hit rock bottom – no one and no company would loan me a dime – God smiled on me. God reminded me of His original call to me, teach his people. In my misery and confusion God reminded me that He had already prepared me for this mission. He reminded me that everything I had gone through was so I could teach with power, spirit, sincerity and truth.

"You can't lead where you don't go and you can't teach what you don't know."
Rev. R.B. Holmes, Jr.

Dr. R.B. Holmes, Jr. is the President of the National Baptist Convention Congress of Christian Education. He is also Senior Pastor of the Bethel Missionary Baptist Church in Tallahassee Florida. One of his favorite sayings is: "You can't lead where you don't go and you can't teach what you don't know."

He reminded me of the importance of a Christian's testimony. He said that a testimony is necessary to win souls to Jesus Christ. (No one wants to go to a heart surgeon who's never operated on anyone before.) In order to have a testimony, I must have successfully experienced some of the things His people are going through. I can truthfully counsel people on divorce – I have been there. I can truthfully counsel people on financial bondage – I have been there. I can truthfully counsel people who feel like giving up on life – I have been there. Now I can truthfully counsel a person who has no one to care for him or her since I have been there. Each time I reached the brink of disaster, I prayed, and God answered and delivered me.

Now I must tell anyone and everyone that God truly cares and He wants all of us to prosper! For as long as I live, I must tell everyone that God loves you. As God spoke to me I began to recognize the parallel in my life and Job's life. He was a perfect and upright man. I still am a born again believer in Jesus Christ. Job was a very wealthy man (Job 1:1-5). I earned more in my first year as a lawyer (more than $250,000) than either of my parents could ever imagine. Then Job lost it all – prestige, money, family and health (Job 1:6-19)! So did I.

I was the first in my family to graduate from high school and college. Because of my financial problems, I felt that I had let my family down. I lost my practice and the prestige of being the first one in my law school class to start a solo law practice. I lost the money that I made because all of my loans were called in. All of my credit cards were canceled for late payments. I had to sell my car – I went from owning a new Infiniti to owning a used, broken down Isuzu with no air conditioning.

People (Christians) I had known over twenty years began to spread vicious rumors about me and they castigated my ministry.
I heard about this from other Christians but I did not hear of any Christians praying for me. Through it all, I kept the faith and I kept tithing.

I lost my family. After 18 years of marriage and two beautiful daughters, I suffered through divorce. The woman I had shared my love, my life and my ministry with since I was 17 years old was gone. Because of being overwhelmed with problems and consumed with bitterness, I gave up and walked out. Then, with no health insurance and a temporary job, I had to undergo two very expensive surgical procedures within a 12-month period. Stress extended my recuperation period and the medical bills were additional bills on top of a sea of debt.

I married briefly for a second time. It was more expensive than the first divorce because it added more debt on top of the mountain of debt I already had. The crumbs I was able to scrape together after the first divorce, I lost with the second one. I was literally broke – utilities and phone disconnected, no groceries, car repossessed and sick children with no health insurance.

Additionally, people (Christians) I had known over twenty years began to spread vicious rumors about me and they castigated my ministry. I heard about this from other Christians but I did not hear of any Christians praying for me. I naively thought the church (fellow church members) would show some compassion and love to my family and me. Unfortunately, all I got was to be the topic of choice for the "gossip committee."

Through it all, I kept the faith and I kept tithing. I kept preaching because God called me to preach and God does not make mistakes. My mistakes were mine. I made them and God had nothing to do with them. How I handled my calling did not distract from God's calling. God is too wise to make a mistake. I did not let anyone separate me from my calling and the love of God.

At the darkest moment of my life, when I literally had only one dollar, I put it in the collection plate. The more desperate my situation became, the more serious my prayers were. It was only when the bottom had fallen out – multiple loss of family, property, reputation, finances and friendships – I fully understood God's true purpose for my ministry. It is to teach God's people through His Word about prosperity. God's purpose was to give me a ministry that I could take to the four corners of the world. **The 90% Rule** can work for anyone, regardless of gender, religion or national origin.

If it would work for a poor black boy born during segregation, from the farm in South Georgia, it will work for anyone, including you. In Asia, America, Africa, Europe, India or Australia, **The 90% Rule** is equally effective. My experience and education were compatible with financial planning, but, like most people, I was deeply in debt. It's not what you know, it's whom you know that will save you – I know Jesus.

God let me understand that my intellect, experience or education could not save me, only the Grace of God. With **The 90% Rule** no prior experience or knowledge is necessary. God is no respecter of persons (Acts 10:34). It does not matter what your knowledge, income or situation are, **The 90% Rule** will work for you.

One of the most fundamental aspects of **The 90% Rule** is a change in attitude. It is like the old adage, "free your mind and your body will follow." **The 90% Rule** says free your wallet and your wealth will follow. A change in attitude is simply saying I do not like where I am financially and I am willing to do something about it NOW! I'm not going to take being poor, broke and hungry ever again! Then make a commitment to live better. I am going to live the life of abundance that Jesus promised (John 10:10). Make this commitment to yourself, your family and your God.

> **"If you are unhappy with your shopping habits learn to always ask yourself three questions before you make any purchase:**
> **Do I want it?**
> **Do I need it?**
> **Can I do without it?"**
> **Barbara Martin**

Ask Before Buying

Barbara Martin, in her book Minimum Wage to Maximum Wealth, provides sound advice for us to consider prior to making purchases. "If you are unhappy with your shopping habits, learn to always ask yourself three questions before you make any purchase: **Do I want it? Do I need it? Can I do without it?** If you are honest with yourself, you'll find that you can answer yes to the last question more times than you might imagine." Try it. You'll be amazed how quickly your financial situation will improve when you think before you act. If you want God to bless you financially, you have to treat your finances as a gift from God. You must honestly think about every purchase and answer those questions first. **You will have a real change in your attitude.**

Affirmation for Wealth

I am in a wealthy place!
I pray daily.
I remember that God has promised me long life and peace.
I trust in the LORD with all my heart and lean not on
my own understanding.
In the name of Jesus Christ, I will never be broke another day in my life!
I am anointed with the wealth favor of God-NOW!

Chapter Six

NOW YOU SEE IT, NOW YOU DON'T

Many people do not worry about tomorrow because they have a good job with good retirement benefits. Consequently, they never plan for the rainy day that will always come. I used to think like this before the bottom fell out on my finances. Governments and businesses alike are "downsizing" and forcing employees to take early retirement. Numerous corporations, during the 1980s, decided to raid their employee pension funds for new sources of production, leveraged buyouts, expansion and operating capital.

In 2001, the $49 billion Enron Corporation became the largest corporate bankruptcy in history, causing tens of thousands to be unemployed and more people lost their pensions. Thousands of stockholders and government pension funds lost billions of dollars when Enron stock

As a rule of thumb, Social Security benefits replace only about a third of a married worker's income (less if you're making more than about $50,000).

went from more than eighty dollars to eighty cents a share. Even Enron's accounting firm, Arthur Andersen – one of the eight largest accounting firms in the world – lost hundreds of millions of dollars due to accounting irregularities for Enron, and, by the time you read this, it may not exist at all. This financial "house of cards" built by Enron devastated the lives and livelihoods of people, the energy (electric, gas, oil, etc.) industry and a major sector of the United States' economy. The fallout still has not settled.

In 2002, World Com, a $36 billion corporation, the largest communications company in the country (30% of the long distance telephone service and 70% of the internet service) followed Enron down the drain – also losing billions for the company, shareholders, investors and confidence in the integrity of American industry. Enron, WorldCom, Adelphia, Global Crossings, K-Mart and Tyco are but some of the multibillion-dollar corporations that went bankrupt in 2001 and 2002. The national and international economic repercussions for retirees, investors, employees and pension funds are still felt and under investigated.

It's unfortunate that the chief executive officers of Enron, WorldCom and others did not heed the advice in **The 90% Rule**. Had they used this sound biblical advice, hundreds of thousands of people would have kept their jobs, millions of shareholders would have had sound investments increasing their wealth and the world economy would have been booming and not looming near disaster. This fact was further highlighted by Simon Romero and Riva D. Atlas, in their recent *New York Times* article entitled, "World Com Files Bankruptcy; Largest U.S. Case". In this article they told us that, "More than half of the 10 biggest bankruptcies since 1980 have occurred in the last 18 months." Listed below are the companies and their pre-bankruptcy assets:

Company	**Year**	**Assets in Billions of Dollars**
WorldCom	2002	$ 107
Enron	2001	63
Texaco	1987	36
Fin. Corp. Am.	1988	34
Global Crossing	2002	26
Adelphia	2002	24
Pacific Gas/Elect.	2001	21
MCorp	1989	20
K-Mart	2002	17
NTL	2002	17

The 90% Rule requires one to get out of debt and live on a "cash-only" basis. It would have saved them time, effort and credibility. More importantly, it would have saved millions of shareholders billions of their hard-earned dollars. "Unlike companies such as WorldCom, US Airways and Vivendi Universal, which have choked on their debt loads, companies that avoided the temptation to borrow during the boom are looking smart." Says Matt Krantz, writing for *USA Today*, in his article entitled. "Companies with no debt fly high," "Now that the economy has slowed, they don't have ominous interest payments that have caused their overaggressive rivals to blow up." He listed the following as the largest debt-free companies in terms of revenue:

- Microsoft
- Walgreen
- Cisco Systems
- Gateway
- Ross Stores
- CDW Computer Centers
- Family Dollar Stores
- Gevity HR

- Bed Bath & Beyond
- C.H. Robinson Worldwide

Through **The 90% Rule** I have told hundreds of individuals about the devastating impact debt has on their lives. Mr. Krantz also reiterates this point in his article when he quotes Peter Andrew, an analyst at A.G. Edwards. "What kills companies is debt," Mr. Andrew said. "Without debt, companies have the financial wherewithal to survive." I think the complete title of this textbook for tithers says it all: **The 90% Rule: How To Get Out of Debt And Prosper, and Why It's Important!**

If all you have at retirement is Social Security, then you will have very little.

Even government pension funds are not immune to losses. During the 1990s, the Orange County, California, government pension fund lost more than one and a half billion dollars (that's billion)! If all you have at retirement is Social Security, then you will have very little. Ms. Martin, in Minimum Wage to Maximum Wealth, makes a profound observation to those who may be unrealistically clinging to the notion that Social Security is their financial salvation. Some people have joined the chorus of "at least I have Social Security."

To begin with, it's important to recognize that Social Security benefits aren't going to put you on Easy Street. As a rule of thumb, Social Security benefits replace only about a third of a married worker's income (less if you're making more than about $50,000). Financial planners generally figure that a family needs 60% to 80%

percent of its gross pre-retirement income to maintain its standard of living after retirement.

That's why we hear of repeated incidents of senior citizens eating cat food because they have very little money for groceries. When you consider how much the elderly have to pay for medicine, it's no wonder they eat cat food. It's the cheapest food available.

Debt is the main reason so many seniors are resorting to eating cat food and having to make a choice of either buying food or medicine. "Once known for their thrift, older Americans are piling on debt – filing for bankruptcy in record numbers and jeopardizing retirement dreams." Stated Christine Dugas in an article for *USA Today*, entitled "American seniors rack up debt like never before," "Many live on little more than Social Security. A sluggish stock market and painfully low interest rates pinch returns on their CDs, bank accounts and stock investments. Tapped out, many in this new generation of seniors turn to credit cards to finance medical bills, expensive prescription drugs and comfortable lifestyles." This new generation of seniors is my generation, the so-called "baby boomers".

The 90% Rule requires you to live initially on 90% of your income. Eventually you should spend no more than 80% of your income for living expenses. This leaves 10% for the church and 10% for your savings. Upon getting your paycheck, give 10% immediately to your church or place of worship. Just as you grow in faith, you should grow in your giving. If you are head over heels in debt, you may not be able to immediately give the full tithe (10%). Begin by giving what you can and build to the tithe, so long as you give consistently.

Organize your finances (budget) to gain control and begin to tithe fully as soon as possible. "*But this I say, He which soweth sparingly shall reap also sparingly; and he which soweth bountifully shall reap also bountifully*" (2 Corinthians 9:6). If you need a financial blessing, you must sow a financial seed. As you give, ask God to direct you in faith, knowledge and resources that will allow you to give fully the portion of your earnings that belong to Him. "*...for God loveth a cheerful giver*" (2 Corinthians 9:7).

I'm a living witness that giving to God is not a chore, but, rather, it is a joy. Once you reach the point where you can joyfully give the tithe, give and do not retreat from it. You will receive a financial blessing when you make a sacrificial financial offering. If you are not a member of a church that believes in Jesus Christ, join one as soon as possible, bring your tithe and see God open the windows of heaven and pour you out a miraculous blessing (Malachi 3:8-12).

Tithe First, Then Pay Yourself

Here's the formula that I follow: after I pay God's tithe (10%), and pay myself, all others follow. After the tithe, take 10% of your remaining income and pay yourself, do this consistently. You deserve to have something for all of your hard work and sacrifice. You may only be able to start with 5%; just start where you are. No one deserves to have your earnings more than you. This can become your savings account. Of course, you should realize that you must have a savings account. Once you have amassed a certain amount in savings, it will become your investment account.

After I pay God His tithe (10%), and pay myself, all others follow.

Later in life, at retirement, this 10% will make the difference between just getting by and living. Instead of eating cat food, you can eat healthy (chicken, fish, steak, etc.) and pay for your prescription medicine. **The 90% Rule** is not some draconian measure to keep you poor. Rather, it is the embodiment of God's goodness for each of us. Although Jesus promised Christians we would live the abundant life, God will not give us His prosperity to waste. Jesus cautioned Christians "*to whom much is given, much is required*" (Luke 12:48). God is blessing us financially such that we can bless His church financially, with our tithes and offerings.

When Ed Koch was mayor of New York City, he used to regularly ask his citizens, "How am I doing?" He obtained a lot of good feedback and provided a number of positive changes to the overall quality of life in the city, from these interactions. Like Mayor Koch, we need to ask ourselves (financially), "How am I doing?" Before you can go anywhere, you have to know where you've been and where you are. Then you can plan for the future and work your future with a plan.

How Am I Doing?

In my moment of soul-searching about my finances I had to ask myself: How am I doing? I think you should do the same. In his book, War on Debt, John Avanzini provides a series of guidelines that helped me determine whether or not I was in the debt trap. If you're in the debt trap, you're in trouble. In essence, it is a financial check-up we should all conduct.

1. **You are in trouble** when you pay more than twenty percent of your gross income on consumer debt.
2. **You are in trouble** when you can only afford to pay the minimum monthly payments on your credit card debt.
3. **You are in trouble** when you start taking those pre-approved credit cards because you have exhausted the current credit limit on the ones you already have.
4. **You are in trouble** when you use credit cards to pay the minimum payment for other credit cards.
5. **You are in trouble** when you make alternating bill payments.

You are in very serious financial trouble, if any of those five situations applies to you.

When I started on this mission in 1985, all of the above applied to me. It is amazing that, when it comes to personal finances, Christians seem no different from the non-Christians. I believe that if we were to take a group of 10 average Americans, Christians or non-Christians, at age 25 and visit them at age 65, only three will have attained financial freedom. The three who will be financially secure will be those who actually live **The 90% Rule**.

Why is it that the prevailing trend in America is for people not to reach financial success? Stephen Leimberg, professor of taxation and estate planning at the American College in Bryn Mawr, Pennsylvania, gives ten reasons why Americans do not attain financial freedom:

1. **They don't know where to start, so they don't**. Beginning is the most important part of

any debt reduction plan. Fear of failure has so petrified some people that they cannot understand financial success is reached by taking one step at a time.

2. **Many have dreams, not goals**. If you are seeking financial security by age 65, you have a dream. However, if you want $1 million by age 65 then you have a goal.
3. **They fear risks**. The few people who have a simple bank account feel secure. This account may be their only asset and investment. A bank account should be looked upon as only one asset in the investment portfolio. Diversification is the key to success during the myriad of economic conditions (inflation, recession, high interest rates, etc.).
4. **They want it all – now**. Only in extremely rare circumstances does a person get rich overnight. If it sounds too good to be true, it usually is.
5. **They don't protect their assets**. While you should never over-insure, you must have adequate life, health, disability income, home and automobile insurance. Additionally, you will need an emergency fund – income, for three to six months.
6. **They can't stay on a financial diet**. In your financial plan, you must allow for a regular practice of saving. Your savings will provide the foundation for your investments. A large number of financial experts advise you to save at least 10% of your income.
7. **They lose sight of the bottom line**. The most important ingredient in your financial plan is the actual money you keep. If you have two investments paying 10%, but the investment

commissions, fees and taxes are higher on one, take the one with the lowest costs.

8. **They use credit poorly**. It is utter nonsense to bank 19 percent of your huge credit card debt while it pays you a mere 5% in your savings account. This 5% is eroded further by taxes, while your credit card debt is further increased by the non-deductibility of its interest. The best thing to do is turn all your credit cards into charge cards. Then pay all the balances on your charge cards each month.
9. **They want others to make them rich**. Only you can make yourself rich!
10. **They give up too easily**. Your goals must be flexible. If you find a short-term goal unmet, just move it to an intermediate-term or long-term goal.

Although Professor Leimberg lists these as reasons why Americans do not attain financial freedom, I think they apply universally. I believe the universal application of these reasons is grounded in the fact that most countries are striving for free market (as in the American free enterprise model) economies.

> **"From this day forward you must consider that you have one great, big payment to make on that big bill."**
> **John Avanzini**

The Bigger they are the Harder the Fall

John Avanzini is one of the most prolific writers in the field of financial prosperity for Christians. He provides practical spiritual warfare techniques to defeat the demon of debt. In Debt Reduction Strategies, he sets out the major strategy needed for anyone wanting to live debt free. In fact, he reveals the key to changing your attitude about debt-free living. The key piece of advice to us is that we must look at all of our bills as if they are combined into one, giant bill.

> "Now don't let the thought of one big bill throw you. It is not as bad as it sounds. Granted, you will now be dealing with your bills as if they are one giant bill, but you will also do the same with your monthly payments. From this day forward you must consider that you have one great, big payment to make on that big bill. This giant payment will consist of the total amount of all your present payments added together."

Mr. Avanzini's perspective is amazing in its simplicity. Everyone, regardless of income or social status, can understand it. Regardless of what country you're from or in, this perspective will work for you. He and other people of God are telling us how God wants us to live.

Everything you do or say is based upon your attitude. In order to get a grip on your personal finances, you must first know how much you owe. Secondly, you must know how much actual income you have. You must know where you are now and where you eventually want to end up. If you do not know where you are headed, financially, chances are you will arrive at the front door of bankruptcy. If you keep on charging, do not save and do not reduce your debt, there is only one place for you: the poorhouse (or, worse yet, "no house").

The Plan To Win

Brothers and sisters, **The 90% Rule** is your plan to win. It allows you to take your individual circumstances and establish a debt-reduction-financial-security plan for your future. It worked for me and I know it'll work for you. The centerpiece of your plan is your budget. Your budget is not some idea or guess; it is a written list of your total income and total expenses for the entire year. You also should write your income statement – income from all sources. Once you get your first paycheck in January, set up your budget – income and expenses – for the entire year (one big bill and one big payment). If you have payroll deductions, for any purposes, list them in your budget. After gathering all this information, set up your monthly payment (remember only one big bill). Once your schedule is set, stick to it and don't change. If it's not in the budget, it can't be spent (for unforeseen expenses, you should have a contingency line item in your budget).

Once you get your first paycheck in January, set up your budget -- income and expenses -- for the entire year (one big bill and one big payment).

If you are not a church member, join a Christian place of worship.

Make the first allocation in your budget a 10 percent payment to your church for tithes. If you are not a church member, join a Christian place of worship. **This 10 percent is the key to your financial success**. It is your reasonable service to God that must be made to attain financial freedom and to overcome the selfishness that, for so many of us, is what got us in this mess to begin with. The second allocation to make in your budget is to pay 10% to yourself in savings. IT TAKES

MONEY TO MAKE MONEY! This savings will provide your emergency money, savings and, later, your investment capital.

The 90% Rule requires you to budget on an annualized basis. That means you must set up your budget for the entire year. Additionally, you must review your spending and account balances each month. This will help you develop a responsible habit of managing your finances. This process allows you to target certain bills for elimination with the goal of becoming debt-free as-soon-as-possible. Adjust your account balances on your statement each month this will let you know which bill is closest to being paid off. Once you become debt-free, you can live on a cash-only basis. **Then make a commitment not to use credit again**. **The 90% Rule** also provides a system of periodic savings for quarterly and annually investing.

Although you may not eliminate all of your debts in one year, you will eliminate some, but, more importantly, you will have embarked upon a spiritual trek toward financial success – freedom from your current financial bondage. **The 90% Rule** will, over time, provide a substantial portion of your available income for savings and investments and still allow you to cover normal expenditures, such as food, utilities, housing and transportation. In the parable that follows, Jesus demonstrates why we must be wise in the use of the financial resources God has blessed us with. To put it in the vernacular, "either use it or lose it!"

After a long time the lord of those servants cometh, and reckoned with them.
And so he that had received the five talents came and brought other five talents, saying

Lord thou deliverest unto me five talents: behold, I have gained beside them five talents more. His lord said unto him, Well done, thou good and faithful servant: thou hast been faithful over a few things, I will make thee ruler over many things: enter thou into the joy of thy lord.

He also that had received two talents came and said, Lord, thou deliverest unto me two talents: behold, I have gained two other talents beside them. His lord said unto him, well done, good and faithful servant; thou has been faithful over a few things, I will make thee ruler over many things: enter into the joy of thy lord.

Then he which had received one talent came and said, Lord, I knew thee that thou art an hard man, reaping where thou has not sown, and gathering where thou has not strawed:

And I was afraid, and went and hid thy talent in the earth: lo, there thou hast that is thine.

His lord answered and said unto him, Thou wicked and slothful servant, thou knewest that I reap where I sowed not, and gather where I have not strawed:

Thou oughtest therefore to have put my money to the exchangers, and then at my coming I should have received mine own with usury.

Take therefore the talent from him, and give it to him which that ten talents.

For unto every one that hath more shall be given, and he shall have abundance: but for him that hath not shall be taken away even that which he hath.

And cast ye the unprofitable servant into outer darkness: there shall be weeping and gnashing of teeth.

(Matthew 25:19-30)

Planning to win allows us to prepare for the 100-fold return, by providing a cash flow management plan. A personal cash flow management system sets up short, intermediate and long-range financial goals. It must also be flexible enough to change with your circumstances. Stanley and Melody Harris, in their book CREDIT REPAIR & MAKING YOUR FINANCES WORK FOR YOU, key in on the significance of time in any personal cash flow management plan. "Time is your greatest ally. The more time you have, the less money you will need to save and invest. The less time you have the more money it will take." **Procrastination is a deadly enemy of your goal to retire with financial dignity!**

Affirmation for Wealth

I am in a wealthy place!
I have written my family's personal financial goals.
I track every dollar coming into and leaving my household.
In the name of Jesus Christ, I will never be broke another day in my life.
I am anointed with the wealth favor of God-NOW!

Chapter Seven

PERSONAL CASH FLOW MANAGEMENT SYSTEM

The 90% Rule requires you to create a Personal Cash Flow Management System. A Personal Cash Flow Management System, if used consistently, can be of great value in helping you gain control of your personal finances. I found its use to be worth its weight in gold. It will ensure that you always have the cash available to pay your bills on time. It also will help you to save more money in a systematic way.

Your cash flow management system will function best if it reflects your goals – whether long-term or

A Personal Cash Flow Management System, if used consistently, can be of great value in helping you gain control of your personal finances.

shor t-term. The purchase of a house in two years or the decision to pay off all of your credit cards by next summer should influence your cash flow management system. The goals you set will provide the framework and schedule for your cash flow management system. Your goals should be your goals (for your specific household) and they should be written so that you may regularly review and pray over them.

The Carter Family Financial Goals

Short Term (within the next year)

- ❑ Pay off all consumer debt $1,000 or less
- ❑ Open a savings account
- ❑ Pay for tuition, books and expenses for college for our daughters

Intermediate Term (within the five years)

- ❑ Begin saving a down payment for a new house
- ❑ Pay off all remaining consumer debt
- ❑ Open an investment account
- ❑ Make an extra car payment each month
- ❑ Purchase a new car for each of our two daughters

Long Term (within the next 10 to 20 years)

- ❑ Buy a new house (paid cash)
- ❑ Prepare and insure an inheritance for our children and their children
- ❑ Go into full-time Christian ministry.

It is important to set aside a portion of each paycheck for your savings and investment program. These funds will come from the accumulation of your 10% savings.

The basic elements of **The 90% Rule**'s Personal Cash Flow Management System are your written annual family budget and your family income statement. They will provide you with the necessary information for a credible cash flow management system that is specific to your family.

I found a cash flow management system to be my best financial friend. It helped me to get the things I wanted, meet my current obligations and saved time and money. It will do the same for you. Another element of the cash flow management system, which I'll discuss later, is your family's written grocery list. Your entire family must understand and be part of your cash flow management system. Everything you earn and spend must be devoted to improving the quality of life for your entire family.

The basic elements of The 90% Rule's Personal Cash Flow Management System are your written annual family budget and your family income statement.

Your cash flow management system also must be suitable for your specific family. Forget the Joneses; your family budget must be workable and understandable by your family – regardless what your friends and neighbors do. It's not only ridiculous to follow the Joneses; it's a sin (Exodus 20:17). You must plan for every contingency – Christmas, birthdays, anniversary presents, vacations, college educations, retirement and emergencies.

After payment of your tithe and your savings, devote your entire remaining income toward household operations and debt reduction. If there is anything left, then you can consider setting aside an amount for entertainment.

You must look at this new giant payment (which is the total for your monthly bills) as a firm financial commitment. **It must be made until every single bill is paid in full.** When one bill is paid, the resulting proceeds should be directed to paying off another until they are all paid. This is the key to debt reduction using **The 90% Rule**.

> **"Nearly 32 cents out of every dollar American families spend is for groceries and household items."**
> **Paul Richard**

Spend Smarter For Grocery and Household

"Nearly 32 cents out of every dollar American families spend is for groceries and household items," says Paul Richard, director of education for the nonprofit National Center for Financial Education (NCFE), based in San Diego, California. The average is three trips a week to the grocery store and one or more stops at a drug or discount store. The NCFE offers the following spending tips to employ before your next trip to the grocery store.

1. **Use a list when shopping.**
2. **Go grocery shopping alone after a meal.**
3. **Watch for store ads in newspaper, your mailbox and flyers distributed at the stores.**
4. **Pay special attention to the days of the week the sale prices are in effect.**
5. **Always spend cash.** Nothing impacts our mind like taking cash from our wallet or purse.
6. **Take advantage of coupons and rebates, they do add up.**
7. **Always shop by the unit price at the stores.** In most states (including Florida)

it's the law that retailers post the unit cost on the shelves.

8. **Avoid buying plastic bags for food storage or garbage disposal.** Most stores give these away free.

9. **Cleaning aids, cleaners, etc., are very costly and prices vary greatly with the brands.** The best cleanser in the kitchen is simple soap powder and ammonia. Another valueless item is dish soap purported to cut grease better and to be gentler on the hands or cuts grease better. If your hands are that sensitive, use the longer lasting rubber gloves and save money on detergent by using generic brands. Hot water and any detergent will cut grease.

10. **Plan meals in advance.** Keep in mind wise use of leftovers and freezing for later use when purchasing meats, etc., and making pasta dishes for example.

11. **Cereals, breads, desserts, juices, beverages, etc., mixed and prepared at home are always a better value than pre-packaged items.**

12. **Be cautious about adding non-food items to the grocery list.** Usually a better value can be obtained at discount drug stores.

13. **When shopping, stick to the list and plan in advance all purchases to take full advantage of sale items and 2 for 1 deals (if the price isn't inflated to compensate).** When possible, shop the outside walls and stay out of the aisles. Most food stores situate the four basics (produce, meats, dairy and bread) on the walls. They most often

place all the cookies, cereals, beverages, canned goods and the nice-to-haves on the aisles.

14. **Finally, check the checker.** Check the register tape again after leaving the store; often-unintentional mistakes are uncovered, especially with large purchases.

As I stated earlier, regarding **The 90% Rule**'s Personal Cash Flow Management System, you must be able to track every dollar coming into your household and every dollar leaving.

Regarding The 90% Rule's Personal Cash Flow Management System, you must be able to track every dollar coming into your household and every dollar leaving.

Every dollar is important and must be accounted for and there must be a legitimate reason to spend each one. Otherwise, it should be put into your savings. Even though groceries are important to the well-being of your family, you also must track every grocery dollar. You must track every grocery dollar because it's easy to waste money at the grocery store. Therefore, you must have a list when you go to the grocery store. Listed on the following page is "THE CARTERS' GROCERY LIST," which my family uses to purchase groceries. **You will need to develop your own family grocery list that is specific to your household and its needs!**

THE CARTERS' GROCERY LIST

Meats
Chicken
Fish
Pork Chops
Turkey Necks
Neck Bones
Hamburger
Sausage
Hot Dogs
Sandwich Meat
Shrimp

Canned/Bottled Goods
Lima Beans
Mushrooms
Pork & Beans
Carrots
Hash
Coffee
Jelly
Mustard
Cooking Oil
Creamer
Soup
Early Peas
Butter Beans
Evaporated Milk
Tang
Peanut Butter
Mayonnaise
Ketchup
Bottled Water
B-B-Que Sauce

Frozen Veggies
Collard Greens
Broccoli
Succotash
Corn on the Cob
Veggie Mix

Pasta/Grains/Cereal/Breads
Rice
Meal
Bread
Grits
Pancake Mix
Cheerios
Flour
Jiffy Mix
Spaghetti
Scalloped Potatoes

Fresh Produce
White Potatoes
Sweet Potatoes
Carrots
Onions
Cabbage
Oranges

Dairy
Milk
Cheese Slices
Block Cheese
Biscuits
Eggs
Margarine
Yogurt
Ice Cream

Snacks
Hi-C Sip Ups
Doritos
Popcorn
Ritz Crackers
Soda
Dinosaurs

Miscellaneous Items
Sugar
Salt
Old Bay
Vitamins
Pepper
Vinegar
Equal/Sweet n Low
Syrup
Garlic Salt
Meat Tenderizer
Crab Boil
Hot Sauce
Worcestershire Sauce
Medications/Prescriptions

Personals
Conditioner
Listerine
Visine
Floss
Soap
Deodorant
Toothpaste
Toothbrushes
Hair Care
Bubble Bath
Perm
Vaseline
Cocoa Butter
Hair Lotion

Eve Wash
Pads/Shields
Q-Tips
Shampoo
Razors
Lotion

Household Items/Paper Ware
Comet
Pine Sol
Dawn
Starch
Carpet Fresh
Powder Bleach
Matches
Toilet Tissue
Ziplock Bags
Sandwich Bags
Coffee Filters
Kleenex
Oven Cleaner
Air Freshener
Air Freshener
Paper Plates
Bathroom Cleaner
Dishwasher Detergent
Laundry Detergent
Dryer Sheets
Vacuum Cleaner BagsDouche
Liquid Bleach
Toilet Freshener
Paper Towels
Baking Bags
Aluminum Foil
Light Bulbs
Furniture Polish
Garbage Bags
Paper Napkins
Paper Napkins
Plastic Forks

School/Office Supplies
Envelopes
Paper
Folders
Stamps
Pencils
Notebooks

Affirmation for Wealth

I am in a wealthy place!
I have a written personal financial plan each year.
I update my personal financial plan each year.
I track all of my spending on a monthly basis.
I have a written budget.
I will spend only what I have budgeted to spend.
In the name of Jesus Christ, I will never be broke another day in my life.
I am anointed with the wealth favor of God-NOW!

Chapter Eight

ORDER OF DEBT REDUCTION

I pray daily for everyone using **The 90% Rule** to be blessed with wealth and prosperity. In fact, I paraphrase a prayer for wealth and prosperity that I heard Creflo Dollar offer. "I am anointed with the wealth favor of God. I'm out of debt, my needs are met, and I have plenty more to put in store and to share." Every day I offer this prayer as an affirmation. In fact, as you read the affirmations before each chapter, you'll see that I have amplified and personalized this powerful affirmation based upon what God has done in my life with **The 90% Rule**.

I pray daily for everyone using The 90% Rule to be blessed with wealth and prosperity.

Using **The 90% Rule**, you'll find that the most basic elements of wealth and prosperity are to eliminate debts and increase the amount of your investments. To do so, you must prioritize your debts. Jesus said that if we seek first God's kingdom and righteousness, He will provide for all our other needs (Matthew 6:33). In essence, we must put "first things first." By putting first things first, you prioritize your debts for liquidation and your savings for accumulation.

In his book, WAR ON DEBT – Breaking the Power of Debt, John Avanzini tells us that we must prioritize our debts for elimination. In your prioritization, target the debts for elimination that will generate the greatest amount of income available as a result. In order to put first things first in your finances, he recommends the following order for elimination of debts:

(1) Credit Card Debt;
(2) Consumer and Installment Loans;
(3) Automobile Loans;
(4) Home Mortgages.

These four categories cover the areas of debts that you may have.

Although you look at all of your debts as one giant bill, you must target specific bills to be paid in the short term, intermediate term and long term. Credit cards are short term, installment loans and car loans are intermediate term, and home mortgages are long-term debts that must be dealt with in a systematic order.

In another of his books, Debt Reduction Strategies, John Avanzini fully explains the concept of systematic debt reduction.

- First, attack your short-term debt. Focus on the bill that will be paid in full in only three months. Suppose its payment is $80. Remember! When this bill is paid, you are not going to have an extra $80 to spend. Instead you are going to have $80 extra to apply to the next bill you target for destruction.
- For example, if you have a bill with a $125 monthly payment that is close to being paid off, add your extra $80 to that bill each month. Even if it takes an extra month or two to pay it off, it is worth waiting in order to have an additional $125 every month to apply toward other bills.

- Here is why, if you pay off a $75 monthly bill, you will have only $155 extra each month ($80 + $75) to apply against the next bill. However, if you pay off the $125 a month bill, you will have $205 extra each month ($80 + $125) to use toward your next bill. With a $205 per month increase in debt reduction money, you will now have a total of $2,460 annually.

This systematic approach also can be successfully applied to your intermediate term and long-term debts.

Money on the Move

Once you've paid off some debts, added the savings to your debt reduction payment and begun a savings account, you're ready to employ other debt reduction strategies. Moving your consumer debts to the lowest available interest rate is a simple debt-reduction strategy. It works exceptionally well in the area of credit card debt.

> **Once you've paid off some debts and added the savings to your debt reduction payment, you're ready to employ other strategies.**

In moving your debt, let me offer you a note of caution. I made a big mistake in changing to a reduced rate credit card without reading all the fine print. A number of national credit card providers offer extremely low (2.9%) introductory rates. I jumped on this offer with both feet. I started out with 2.9 % and ended up six months later with 18.99%. Like the Apostle Paul says, "I would not have ye be ignorant brethren" so, please check the fine print on these discount rate credit cards before signing up.

Begin by checking with each of the lending institutions that have issued you credit cards. You'll want to know which card charges the lowest annual interest fee. When determining which is the lowest, you also should take into consideration any additional fees charged by that lender – costs such as annual fees, annual interest rates (including introductory rates), transaction fees, establishing other accounts and so on. Also check with your credit union. If you are not a member, maybe you should join. Generally most credit union interest rates and fees are less costly than banks, but always check the facts.

Mr. Avanzini continues his wise counsel in Debt Reduction Strategies: "Once you've successfully moved your credit card debt to the lowest possible interest rate, under no circumstances must you allow yourself to pay the lower minimum monthly payment that comes with your new, lower-interest-rate credit card debt." That's why you must use the entire amount of your savings from bills paid off only for debt reduction. Keep your monthly payment at least as large as it was before you moved your debt. When you do this, you will find you not only have lower total debt to pay because you owe less interest, but you also have a higher principal payment to more rapidly reduce the debt. Continue to pay the higher payment causes your restructured credit card debt to pay off much faster.

"During the final months of your master plan payoff, you will be paying bills off in one month that would have taken as long as a year at the minimum payments."
John Avanzini

There is another way to move your debt to a lower interest rate. You can pay off all your bills by placing a new, second mortgage on your home. With the current tax structure, this is the best tax deduction available to all homeowners. Today these loans are more commonly called home equity loans and are offered by banks, savings and loan associations and mortgage companies. Remember, if you decide on this course of action, the new loan must be large enough to totally pay off all of your outstanding debts. Stay with **The 90% Rule** and use all savings from liquidated debts to pay that one giant bill!

A Deal Behind the Wheel

There's an old adage that "if you buy a used car, you're buying someone else's junk." Therefore, you should always buy a new car, if possible. However, some people regularly purchase "previously owned vehicles" or "off-lease vehicles" and have experienced favorable results. Then there are people like me who are not mechanically inclined and have nothing but bad experiences with used cars. There is something very important about your automobile that you must keep in mind. No matter how good it is, it will eventually wear out. This means you must have a perpetual plan of action to replace your present car. Vehicles tend to wear out or become too expensive to maintain within five to six years. If you don't get at least 100,000 miles from your new car, then you didn't get a good one or you didn't keep up with normal maintenance (oil change, tune ups, etc.).

"During the final months of your master plan payoff, you will be paying bills off in one month that would have taken as long as a year at the minimum payments," wrote John Avanzini in Debt Reduction Strategies. There also will be a day when you can apply the entire amount (excluding your mortgage payment) each month to your automobile loan. This will allow you to pay off the car in only a few months instead of the remaining three of four years that the regular payment would have taken.

The House Down the Street

When the entire amount of monthly income is available, why not take four or five hundred dollars from your regularly monthly spending, then apply the extra $900 to $1,000 each month to your home mortgage. In just a few more years, you will really be debt free.

When you consider "the house down the street", make sure it's the right house for your family. Location is the most important consideration to make when buying a house. Try to buy in a subdivision where most houses are more expensive than yours. When your house is the least expensive in the subdivision, the higher priced homes will tend to pull up its value. Just the opposite will take place if you buy the most expensive house in a subdivision. Also, try to buy a house big enough to meet your needs for at least 10 years. Therefore, if you're a young couple just starting out and planning to have children, you should buy a three-bedroom house rather than a one-bedroom house.

Regardless of what size house you buy or what neighborhood you move into, plan to pay off the entire mortgage.

Regardless of what size house you buy or what neighborhood you move into, plan to pay off the entire mortgage. When you buy a house, you're making a long-term commitment to live in a community. Just because you've made a long-term commitment to the community doesn't mean you've made a long-term commitment to the mortgage company. Pay off your mortgage as soon as possible. I believe I have an awesome God for whom nothing is too hard (Genesis 18:14).

Of all the spiritual insights on debt reduction I got from the many books of John Avanzini that I've read, the "unspecified principal-reduction strategy" was worth its weight in gold.

Of all the spiritual insights on debt reduction I got from the many books of John Avanzini that I've read, the "unspecified principal-reduction strategy" was worth its weight in gold. The unspecified principal-reduction strategy is a mortgage payment strategy with the most possibilities. This is the strategy that we are using to pay off our 30-year mortgage in twelve years. This is because it has no specified amount that will be prepaid. That amount can be from one cent over the regular payment, all the way to the entire amount of the unpaid balance. It can be a one-time payment, a monthly payment, an annual payment or any combination of these.

The flexibility of this strategy is unlimited. It can be adjusted to your changing financial needs and circumstances. If you receive periodic bonuses or tax refunds, they can be added to your regular payment. (We are making two payments a month, plus $100 extra.) Every time any extra amount is paid, it will shorten the term of the note. It also will cause an interest cost reduction.

SUPPORT INFORMATION

The Unspecified Principal-Reduction Strategy
10.5% Interest Rate

Illustration 1
Making an additional $100 Principal Payment Each Month

Loan Amount	$100,000.00
Term	30 Years
Payment	$914.74
Extra Payment Amount	$100.00

Payment No.	Interest	Principal	Extra Payment	Balance
1	$875.00	$39.74	$100.00	$99,860.26
2	873.78	40.96	100.00	99,719.30
3	872.54	42.20	100.00	99,577.10
4	871.30	43.44	100.00	99,433.66
5	870.04	44.69	100.00	99,288.97
6	868.78	45.96	100.00	99,143.01
7	867.50	47.24	100.00	98,995.77
8	866.21	48.53	100.00	98,847.24
9	864.91	49.83	100.00	98,697.42
10	863.60	51.14	100.00	98,546.28
	Payments 11 through 221 omitted to conserve space.			
222	48.10	866.64	100.00	4,530.07
223	39.64	875.10	100.00	3,554.97
224	31.11	883.63	100.00	2,571.33
225	22.50	892.24	100.00	1,579.09
226	13.82	900.92	100.00	578.17
227	5.06	578.17	0.00	0.00

SAVINGS WITH THIS STRATEGY:
Interest – $98,377.10 Time – 11 yrs.

“Good Hands” or “Good Neighbors”

Mr. Avanzini, in WAR ON DEBT – Breaking the Power of Debt, continues to provide gems of wisdom, including such personal matters as insurance. **The 90% Rule** recognizes the need for family protection and surety against property loss. The type and amount of insurance needed is based upon your particular family’s financial needs. No matter what type of insurance you need, there are several things you must consider before you buy. Remember, whatever you save in premiums should be used to pay down your debt.

The 90% Rule recognizes the need for family protection and surety against property loss.

Mr. Avanzini advises that these considerations should be made before buying insurance:

1. **To the best of your ability, determine exactly how much insurance you need.**
2. **Always shop around for the best buy.**
3. **Never let your agent decide what you should buy.**
4. **Always buy the highest deductible you can afford to pay.**
5. **Never buy a policy you don’t understand.**
6. **Whenever possible, make your premium payments once a year.**
7. **Don’t be afraid to investigate a prospective insurance company.**
8. **Every time you renew your policy, or at least once a year, re-evaluate your coverage to be sure it still meets all your needs.**

A Living Soul

"And the LORD God formed man of the dust of the ground, and breathed into his nostrils the breath of life; and man became a living soul" (Genesis 2:7). When God made us, He made each one of us "a living soul". When you recognize that you are a living soul, you will become **God-Inside Minded**. To be God-Inside Minded is to recognize that you are more than just "Joe Lunch Bucket." You are very special because you are made in the image of God. **The 90% Rule** provides you with a new attitude to recognize that you are a child of God. Now that you have recognized a change in your attitude, you can increase your financial altitude. It's time to start thinking wealth and prosperity. It is time for you to start thinking about how much God wants you to have the best that life has to offer.

> **Once you get your mind right (I am debt free), you are already on the road to financial recovery.**

You cannot afford the best unless you change your mind about debt. Your attitude should focus on being the best that you can be for yourself and your family. Once you get your mind right (I am debt-free), you are already on the road to financial recovery. Now you need a plan, in essence a road map, to complete your journey.

Just as the Bible is a spiritual guide through life, you need a financial guide to lift you from the quagmire of debt. **The 90% Rule** has shown you how to prepare your personal cash flow management system, which is your plan to win. The pages immediately following provide a sample budget and income statement to guide you through making your own budget.

The 90% Rule

SAMPLE PERSONAL CASH FLOW MANAGEMENT PLAN

CURRENT BUDGET

Creditor	Interest Rate	Monthly Payment	Account Balance
YOUR CHURCH			
YOUR SAVINGS			
MORTGAGE			
GROCERIES			
UTILITIES			
CHILD CARE			
TELEPHONE			
DISCOVER			
J C PENNEY			
DEPARTMENT STORE			
MASTERCARD			
ALLSTATE			
STATE FARM			
VISA			
ENTERTAINMENT			
TOTALS			

The 90% Rule

SAMPLE BUDGET

Net Annual Income: $28,068.76

Expenses (Creditor)

Payment Schedule	**Interest Rate**	**Monthly Payment**	**Account Balance**
Your Church (tithes)	N/A	$233.91	$2,806.87
Savings (10%)	2.5%	233.91	2,806.87
Mortgage or Rent	8.5%	600.00	7,200.00*
Car Payment	12%	375.00	4,500.00
Utilities	N/A	150.00	1,800.00
Phone	N/A	35.00	420.00
Groceries	N/A	320.00	3,840.00
Insurance (Life)	N/A	35.00	420.00
Insurance (Car)	N/A	50.00	600.00
Insurance (Health)	N/A	50.00	600.00
Insurance (Homeowner)	N/A	40.00	480.00
Mastercard	18.9%	41.67	500.00
Visa	22.9%	66.67	800.00
Dillards	20.5%	25.00	300.00
Sears	12%	20.83	250.00
Discover	18%	20.83	250.00
Chevron	18%	30.00	360.00
B.P./Gulf	18%	40.00	480.00
Furniture	20%	41.67	500.00
Entertainment	N/A	**46.54**	**558.56**
TOTALS		**$2,339.07**	**$28,068.76**

*Annual amount of rental or mortgage payments. Principal balance on mortgage is not shown.

The 90% Rule

SAMPLE INCOME STATEMENT

INCOME SOURCE	NET INCOME AMOUNT	INCOME SCHEDULE
State of Florida	$ 1,905.73	Monthly
(Administrative Assistant II Pay Grade 18)	$ 22,868.76	(Annually)
WalMart	$ 100.00	Weekly
(Part-time 20 hours/week)	$ 5,200.00	(Annually)
TOTAL ANNUAL NET INCOME:	**$ 28,068.76**	**($2,339.06)***

*This amount represents annual salary divided by 12.

Affirmation for Wealth

I am in a wealthy place!
I trust in godly counsel.
I seek godly counsel regarding my finances.
I am blessed (empowered to prosper) and happy because I do not live
according to the counsel of the ungodly, nor do I live by their advice,
plans or purposes.
My delight is in the law of the LORD and I will habitually meditate on His
Word day and night for instructions and guidance.
I am anointed with the wealth favor of God-NOW!

Chapter Nine

THE TEN PERCENT SOLUTION

Jesus reminds us that the encapsulation of our life's mission is to love God with all our heart, soul, mind and might (Mark 12:30). Hence, pay God before paying any other creditor as part of the first great commandment. The second is also like this, in that we are required to love our neighbors as ourselves. The underlying presumption in Jesus' words is that we love ourselves.

The 90% Rule offers the Ten Percent Solution based on the Word of God. The Ten Percent Solution is our way of demonstrating that we love ourselves.

The Ten Percent Solution is our way of demonstrating that we love ourselves. Therefore, after we have given our reasonable financial service (10%) to God, we are to give our reasonable financial service (10%) to ourselves.

Therefore, after we have given our reasonable financial service (10%) to God, we are to give our reasonable financial service (10%) to ourselves. All other creditors fall in line afterwards.

The Scriptures tells us not to "muzzle" the ox that treads out the corn (1 Timothy 5:18). As the person who is working to earn the income necessary to operate a household, meet financial obligations and provide a quality of life, you are also entitled to payment. In essence, don't kill the goose that lays the golden eggs because, if you do, there will be no eggs. We need the eggs! We cannot begin to accumulate wealth and attain our preferred lifestyle unless we practice the Ten Percent Solution.

Another part of not muzzling the ox is for families not to fight over money. It should be a joint commitment for debt-free living. It should be a joint commitment on how to get there. If one spouse is better equipped to handle the day-to-day family finances, it should be a joint commitment for that person to do so. The entire process (knowing what's going on in your family finances) must be transparent.

The monthly statement reviews should be a joint activity so that both spouses can know where they are financially on a timely basis. Before **The 90% Rule**, my wives and I didn't totally share financial information with each other. We each had our respective accounts. I had no idea what they were doing and they had no idea what I was doing financially.

You've read in the earlier chapters of this book the results of this approach – chaos, broken dreams and frustrations that followed in my life. Currently we have established a main household account (mortgage, insurance, utilities, tuition, etc.) that I am the primary manager for. Additionally, she has her individual checking account and so do I. The individual accounts are for personal non-budget items. This separation of accounts is possible but there must be a coming together on how to get there (financial security) and both parties must be kept informed. Each month, we review the budget, account balances and income statements.

The Ten Percent Solution is **The 90% Rule**'s systematic and on-going savings plan. The proceeds from this savings plan will be used as the foundation for an investment portfolio. Do not be discouraged if you have only $10 or less currently available to save monthly. Most credit unions and some banks have what they call Christmas Clubs, which allow for lower initial deposits and minimal regular deposits throughout the year. The important step is to begin saving now.

The savings account that you establish will serve as one component of your overall investment portfolio. Regardless of your age and the amount you have available, a systematic on-going savings account will benefit you. The key thing to remember is to START SAVING NOW! The time value of money (money saved today is worth more in the future) will greatly benefit you. If you save only $10 per month, at the end of the year you will have $120. You will begin the next year with your $120 plus the interest it earned. If you follow **The 90% Rule** for that year, you may have an additional $10 or more each month to save. The goal is to consistently save a certain amount each month.

A note of caution is warranted here. Your savings account should be your savings account, not your emergency fund.

A note of caution is warranted here. Your savings account should be your savings account, not your emergency fund. For emergencies, illnesses, etc., you should utilize your insurance and/or your budget allocation for contingency expenses. If at all possible, do not disturb your savings. The continuous savings plan is necessary in order to fund your investment portfolio. Your investment portfolio is necessary to keep you debt free in the future and increase your lifestyle choices. Additionally, in order to invest, you will need some funds. ("It takes money to make money.")

Once you have saved at least $3,000.00, you are ready to begin an investment program. What should you invest in? In a word – property! The best way to invest in property is to diversify. There are two types of property: personal and real. Property can be both tangible (i.e., real estate) and intangible (stocks, bonds). All property investments fall within those two categories. At the beginning of each year, when you are establishing your personal cash flow management system (i.e., your annual budget), review the total amount saved, complete your income tax filing (whatever refund you anticipate should be added to savings) and research investment opportunities.

I feel it's incredible to constantly demand that Christian members meet their financial obligations (tithes and offerings) without telling them how to obtain the necessary financial resources to meet all of their responsibilities.

The two types of property include all types of investments. It is up to you to determine what investments you actually will make. The types of investments also will depend upon the amount of funds you have available. It also will depend on what you are most comfortable investing in. Always contact an investment counselor before investing. The key to any investment portfolio is diversification – never put all your eggs in one basket. If something happens to that one basket, all the eggs are gone. Remember, we need the eggs!

There are also other recommendations for investment portfolios. As your investment funds and needs grow, you should seek a professional investment counselor. Most full-service brokerage firms (i.e., Merrill Lynch; American Express etc.) offer quality advice and a full range of investment opportunities. Unless you have some knowledge about investments and are doing your own research, beware of discount or "do-it-yourself" brokerages.

For years I have been frustrated. I have seen certain Christian church leaders become out of touch with their congregations by making them feel guilty about tithes and offerings. I feel it's incredible to constantly demand that Christian members meet their financial obligations (tithes and offerings) without telling them how to obtain the necessary financial resources to meet all of their responsibilities.

God did not command that you give your mortgage payment to the church. He asked that you bring your tithes and offerings. With church leaders like this, I often think of Pharaoh, who demanded that the children of Israel make the same number of bricks but withheld the straw necessary to make them. The Apostle Paul reminds us "*God shall supply all of (our) needs according to His riches in glory by Christ Jesus*" (Philippians 4:19).

God's riches in glory mean that He will give you all that you need when you need it. The message to the believer is to come to God for your every need; if you're broke, remember that Jesus came that we may have a more abundant life (John 10:10). We don't go to church to get beat up, chewed out or browbeaten. We go to church to get lifted up.

That means that the church can legitimately compel you to pay your tithes and bring your offerings after it has shown you how to make your ends meet. **The 90% Rule** is a spiritual tool for the church to help you get a grip on your personal finances, earn a decent living for your family and meet your obligations to the Most High God. In addition to teaching you the biblical method for debt reduction through **The 90% Rule**, we also may be able to assist you with professional financial counseling.

There are also a number of qualified independent financial planners that can assist you. Some professional financial planners do not invest for you, they make recommendations (i.e., develop financial plans, identify financial goals, etc.). There are others who provide financial counseling, investment advice and assistance and business opportunities. I recently spoke to a regional vice president for Primerica Financial Services, regarding **The 90% Rule**, and as an advisor and investment counselor, he offered me the following advice: "A person should plan [financially] for their living and for their [families in] dying."

Debt Counselors Are Not The Same

Christine Dugas, writing for *USA Today*, cautions us to beware in seeking debt counseling, in her article entitled: "All debt counselors are not the same." Because of the tremendous debt load Americans are carrying, there has been a boom in the growth of debt counseling agencies. "Certainly there is a need. Consumer debt loads continue to mount. More credit card holders are falling behind on payments. The number of Americans filing for bankruptcy hit a record 1.45 million last year." Ms Dugas said.

As an advisor for The 90% Rule and investment counselor, let me offer you some sound advice: "A person should plan (financially) for their living and for their (families in) dying."

"Ideally, consumers should consult a debt counselor well before they are ready to file for bankruptcy. But even when they do, they are not always well-served because the quality of the counseling services varies considerably. There are no uniform federal licensing requirements. Only 17 states have laws regarding them."

I was particularly pleased with Ms. Dugas' article because I have been saying the same thing for more than 10 years. "There are many reputable credit counselors. The best offer a range of services, including debtor education, budget counseling and debt management programs." Ms. Dugas stated.

This sums up the purpose of **Part I of The 90% Rule** that provides an answer to the following question: How To Get Out Of Debt And Prosper? By arming you with this information, you can develop your personal plan for getting out of debt or, when speaking to a credit counselor, know the components of a quality and sound debt reduction plan.

I have found quality Christian advice and counsel to be invaluable in my personal investment program. Any true professional counselor will need to provide a comprehensive financial analysis for a person before advising him or her on a financial plan. A quality counselor never recommends any investments before providing a financial evaluation. **It's important to have some idea as to where you are before deciding where you are going.**

PART II:
HOW TO OBTAIN WEALTH AND PROSPERITY!

Affirmation for Wealth

I am in a wealthy place!
I do not waste the finances God has placed in my care.
I am debt-free.
I invest in different types of investments to ensure my family's future.
In the name of Jesus Christ, I will never be broke another day in my life.
I am anointed with the wealth favor of God-NOW!

Chapter Ten

INVESTING FOR WEALTH

By now you know that you need a savings program. **The 90% Rule** recommends that you begin by saving at least 5% of your income. This is not your "ready-cash" and/or emergency fund. You need to have a line item in your personal cash management system for "contingencies" that will perform this function. By living **The 90% Rule** you eventually should be able to save between 5% and 15% of your income.

> **Eventually you should save between 5% and 15% of your income. All that you save over 5% should be put aside into an investment account.**

All of your income that you save over 5% should be put aside into an investment account. You will need to have at least $3,000 to begin an investment program. Remember: 5% should remain as your savings account. There are multiple wealth building components to **The 90% Rule**, they include:

(1) A commitment to tithing, since the tithe belongs to God and is Holy;
(2) A commitment to a regular savings plan;
(3) A commitment to live on a written budget;
(4) A commitment to prayer and daily affirmations for wealth and prosperity; and

(5) A commitment to support worldwide Christian evangelism and give offerings.

It does not hurt to give to the Christian church if you don't have to choose between supporting God's church and feeding your family. **The 90% Rule** provides you with a mechanism to avoid this conflict. Also, you can give more when you earn more.

When I started Carter Ministries, Kenneth Copeland's words resounded in my spirit. He said, the "purpose of ministry is to meet the needs of God's people". In my prayer, fasting, and meditation I remembered my calling. God called me into ministry with a mission. Therefore, He gave me **The 90% Rule** that provides an answer to the question: **How to get out of debt and prosper and why**?

> **God called me into ministry with a mission. Therefore, He gave me The 90% Rule that provides an answer to the question: How to get out of debt and prosper and why?**

I've spent Part I of this book teaching you how to get out of debt and why. Getting out of debt is necessary when you consider how many Christians are in debt and how long they've been in debt. You didn't get "head over heels" in debt overnight and you're not going to get out overnight. If you follow **The 90% Rule**, you'll not only get out of debt, you'll stay out.

In Part II of this book, I want to show you how you can obtain wealth and prosperity. This is the other fundamental perspective of **The 90% Rule**, teaching you how to prosper. Debt reduction and wealth accumulation go hand-in-hand.

Your investment percentages should reflect your age, temperament, goals and the amount of risk you are comfortable with.

Now you are ready for a general review of investments. It makes no sense to get out of debt just to get right back into it. After you get out of debt, it's time to maintain and increase your wealth such that you can be a blessing to the body of Christ. In essence, you can give out of your overflow of wealth and bless so many more churches, missions and those less fortunate. I should caution you again about investments. Before investing, you should pray, research and seek professional help.

Listed on the next page are the diversified components of **The 90% Rule**'s Sample Investment Portfolio. For each component there is the recommended percentage each should constitute in the sample portfolio. (NOTE: Those percentages are based on a typical family of four with the head of the household age 45. Your percentages should reflect your age, temperament, goals and the amount of risk with which you are comfortable. Please seek professional help prior to making any investments.)

The 90% Rule – Sample Investment Portfolio

Bonds and/or bond Mutual Funds – 33%

- Government
- Corporate
- Mortgage

Cash – 1%

- Bank Savings Account
- Money Market Account
- Certificates of Deposit
- U.S. Savings Bonds
- Treasury Bills

Collectibles – 1%

- Antiques
- Coins
- Stamps

Insurance – 1%

- Life (Term, Universal Life, Whole Life)
- Health
- Disability
- Property and Casualty

Real Estate – 15%

- Home
- Residential
- Commercial
- Lease Purchase Agreements
- Real Estate Investment Trusts
- Raw (undeveloped) Land

Stock and/or Stock Mutual Funds – 45%

- Growth
- Income
- International

The percentages do not reflect the value of these components; rather they represent the actual dollars invested.

Larry Burkett, in his book, Investing During Your Middle Years, provides a Christian perspective on investing. It's important to take the financial resources yielded from your use of **The 90% Rule** and invest them for your current and future financial needs. I believe that the counsel Larry Burkett offers in his book provides the "wisdom of God" necessary for Christian investing.

When you read his book, pay particular attention to his investment principles. They are:

1. **Diversification** (Ecclesiastes 11:2). Divide your investment capital into several different types of investment vehicles – "Don't put all your eggs in one basket."
2. **Ethical Investing** (Ecclesiastes 12:13) "Is what I am about to do going to be pleasing to the Lord?" If not, stay away from it – no matter what the potential profit.
3. **Good Counsel** (Proverbs 15:22) "Good counsel is essential to good planning." A good Christian investment counselor is not only a good (decent, nice) person but also a competent professional.

Child of God, it does little good for you to pay God the tithe, establish a saving account and become debt-free just to fall into debt all over again. The Word of God tells us that we must get an understanding and appreciation of his wisdom (Proverbs 4:7). Remember the ultimate goals of **The 90% Rule** are to provide you the biblical method for becoming debt-free and provide you with wealth and prosperity.

A major benefit to you for using **The 90% Rule** is that your faith will be strengthened. "*Now faith is the substance of things hoped for, the evidence of things not seen*" (Hebrews 11:1). As you begin this journey, you must believe in your core being (the depths of your heart) that you can become debt-free and live a life of prosperity. I know that if you truly embrace (via prayer, study, faith and meditation) the biblical principles and spiritual insights of **The 90% Rule**, you will become prosperous and have good success (Joshua 1:8).

Investor's Business Daily 10 Secrets of Success

There are a lot of practical affirmations and guidelines that amplify the spiritual perspective of **The 90% Rule**. *Investor's Business Daily*'s 10 Secrets of Success is one set of those practical guidelines that you may find helpful. I have found *Investor's Business Daily* to be one of the premier investment publications available, providing qualitative research and practical insights on businesses and investments. They have spent years analyzing leaders and successful people in all walks of life.

1. **HOW YOU THINK IS EVERYTHING**: Always be positive. Think success, not failure. Beware of a negative environment.
2. **DECIDE UPON YOUR TRUE DREAMS AND GOALS**: Write down your specific goals and develop a plan to reach them.
3. **TAKE ACTION**: Goals are nothing without action. Don't be afraid to get started. Just do it.

4. **NEVER STOP LEARNING**: Go back to school or just read books. Get training and acquire skill.
5. **BE PERSISTENT AND WORK HARD**: Success is a marathon, not a sprint. Never give up.
6. **LEARN TO ANALYZE DETAILS**: Get all the facts, all the input, learn from your mistakes.
7. **FOCUS YOUR TIME AND MONEY**: Don't let other people or things distract you.
8. **DON'T BE AFRAID TO INNOVATE**: Be different: Following the herd is a sure way to mediocrity.
9. **DEAL AND COMMUNICATE WITH PEOPLE EFFECTIVELY**: No person is an island. Learn to understand and motivate others.
10. **BE HONEST AND DEPENDABLE**: Take responsibility: Otherwise, Numbers 1-9 won't matter.

Most have these 10 traits but when combined they can turn dreams into reality.

Interest Rates

The Federal Reserve continued to "slash interest rates in another bid to stimulate a stalled economy," according to Barry Flynn. Mr. Flynn, staff writer for the *Orlando Sentinel* newspaper, wrote an article dealing with interest rates entitled "Latest Fed move cuts both ways". In the article, he gave us a historical glance at interest rates that showed the interest rates reduction to 2% is the lowest since 1961. This was actually the tenth time in 2001 that the Federal Reserve had lowered interest rates.

The Federal Reserve began an aggressive series of rate cuts in 2001 to deal with the major downturn in the economy and to encourage economic activity by reducing borrowing costs. Sir Isaac Newton's theory of equilibrium states that "for every action there is an equal and opposite reaction." In the article, Mr. Flynn also uses a subtitle, "Low rates are no bargain for retirees, savers." In essence, the opposite reaction hurts a segment of our society.

The plunging interest rates also have slashed the income of millions of retirees whose lifestyles and well-being depend on fixed-rate investments – certificates of deposit, money market accounts and bonds. In the final analysis, some economists are seeing the results of the latest interest rate cuts as a possible "worst case scenario" in the economy.

Federal Reserve Short Term Interest Rates for 2001

Date	**Amount**	**Rate**
January 9	½ point	6%
January 31	½ point	5.5%
March 20	½ point	5%
April 20	½ point	4.5%
May 15	½ point	4%
June 27	¼ point	3.75%
August 21	¼ point	3.5%
September 17	½ point	3%
October 2	½ point	2.5%
November 6	½ point	2%

As I stated earlier, **The 90% Rule** will work for anyone, regardless of race, gender, age or national origin. Additionally, **The 90% Rule** works in any economy because it is based on the Word of God and not the business cycles in the economy.

It is possible for any person to get out of debt and prosper using the biblical principles of **The 90% Rule**. During 2001, *Black Enterprise* magazine ran a special series on wealth accumulation for African Americans. Carolyn M. Brown, writing for Black Enterprise in this series called "Black Wealth Initiative," provided insight on wealth and prosperity with a declaration of financial independence. Can you make this pledge? I have. It will make a difference for all peoples!

Declaration of Financial Empowerment

From this day forward, I declare my vigilant and lifelong commitment to financial empowerment. I pledge the following:

1. To save and invest 10% to 15% of my after-tax income.
2. To be a proactive and informed investor.
3. To be a disciplined and knowledgeable consumer.
4. To measure my personal wealth by net worth, not income.
5. To engage in sound budget, credit and tax management practices.
6. To teach business and financial principles to my children.
7. To use a portion of my personal wealth to strengthen my community.
8. To support the creation and growth of profitable, competitive [Christian]-owned enterprises.

9. To maximize my earning power through a commitment to career development, technological literacy and professional excellence.
10. To ensure that my wealth is passed to future generations.

Notwithstanding racism, sexism and all the other "isms," **The 90% Rule** will help you obtain wealth and a life of prosperity.

At the end of each year, you should update your personal financial statement. As you work through the statement you will be able to ascertain your net worth (how much you have after deducting how much you owe). You should date the form, sign it and place it with your other financial records (will, annual budget, tax forms, property deeds, etc.). By using **The 90% Rule**, you should see an increase in your financial net worth each year.

Your Credit History

Just as you go to your doctor to get an annual physical examination, you should have an annual financial examination as well. As you reduce your overall debt

For a complete picture of your credit history, you need to get a report from each of the major credit-reporting companies.

service, you should review your credit report annually. You must know everything possible about your financial net worth, including your creditworthiness. Each year you must review your personal credit report to ensure its accuracy and to make sure it reflects those bills you have paid in full. You should make this check regardless of whether you have been turned down for credit. If you discover any inaccuracies, you have a right to correct them.

For a complete picture of your credit history, you need to get a report from each of the major credit-reporting companies. Because retailers and credit-card companies are affiliated with one of the three reporting systems, the reports often contain different information. When requesting a copy of your report, include your full name with first name, middle initial, last name and Jr., Sr. or other suffix if it's appropriate (i.e., John F. Jones, Sr.). You also need to supply your date of birth, your Social Security number and your last few addresses.

"You Can't Get Credit Unless You Already Have Credit"

Credit is like a "Catch 22"; you can't get it unless you already have it. However, if you follow the recommendations of **The 90% Rule** you will be able to qualify for credit. Once you qualify for credit, then you'll have a credit history. When it comes to your credit history, what you don't know can hurt you. When a creditor (bank, credit card issuer, mortgage company, etc.) looks at you, do you know what they are looking for? Generally, all creditors look at you from the standpoint of the "three C's of credit". The three C's of credit determine your creditworthiness. They are: Character, Collateral and Capacity.

The three C's of credit determine your creditworthiness. They are: Character, Collateral and Capacity.

Character tells creditor basic information, albeit important information, about you. This basic information includes: your age, employment, residence (rent or own, duration at the address), savings, investment or insurance. Collateral tells a creditor what things you own that you are willing to risk to secure the credit. Collateral includes your home, other property, automobile, savings or other things of value.

Like Character and Collateral, Capacity is also very important. Capacity tells a creditor how much you can pay based on your current financial situation. That means they look at how much you have in income from all sources, what your current monthly expenses are and what amount, if any, you have after you have paid your current expenses. In essence, can you handle another payment?

Before venturing down to your local bank for a loan, you may want to know where you stand based upon the "three C's." One easy way to do so is to review your personal credit report. A major component of **The 90% Rule** is to conduct an annual review of your credit report. As I stated earlier, when it comes to your credit history, what you don't know can hurt you. At the least, a credit-report blemish could keep you from getting a department-store-credit card or car loan. At worst, it could kill your chances of getting a mortgage or certain sensitive jobs. That's not all. The credit problem that scotches your car loan may not even be yours.

A major component of The 90% Rule is to conduct an annual review of your credit report . . . when it comes to your credit history, what you don't know can hurt you.

For those of you who like to apply for every credit card special offered by a department store ("free gift, if you sign up for a charge card") or receive unsolicited in the mail, a word of caution. Each time there is an inquiry in your credit, regardless of the outcome, it's recorded in your credit report. Multiple inquiries are recorded negatively, depending on the frequency, regardless of whether you receive the card or not.

Remember to check out your report because countless others will do so. The U.S. Fair Credit Reporting Act (FCRA) regulates who can see your credit reports. In general, credit card companies, lenders, some employers and insurers have access to the reports. You have a right to know as much about your credit report as strangers in far away places in countless corporations.

When a person is denied credit, the company must identify which of the credit reports it relied on in making a decision.

It's a complex national information exchange where mortgage companies, retailers like Sears, Macys, J. C. Penney's and other credit-card issuers tell credit checkers about their experiences with customers. Does the customer pay on time? How many times has the payment been late? What's the current balance on the account? What's the highest it has ever been? The reports also include basic information including current and past addresses and employers and certain information filed in public records (e.g. mortgages, liens, etc.).

The FCRA also sets up an elaborate procedure for consumers to find out about and fix errors in their credit files. When a person is denied credit, the company must identify which of the credit reports it relied on in making a decision. That company must also send you a copy of the credit report it used to base its decision on. Another federal law, the Equal Credit Opportunity Act, also forces the company to divulge why a person was turned down.

If you're not satisfied by the outcome of the FCRA procedure, you can complain to the Federal Trade Commission (FTC), which regulates the credit-reporting industry. In addition to a letter outlining your dispute, you should send the FTC a copy of the letter declining to offer you credit and any available documentation. Send it to the FTC office in Washington, DC.

A Note of Caution

The 90% Rule also requires you to check your credit report because someone may purposely use your credit report for criminal reasons. It's extremely important that you review your credit report each year to see if there are any irregularities. If there are any irregularities, this annual check will allow you to identify them in a timely

That's why you need to know what's in your credit report and you need to know as soon as possible.

manner. Within the last three years, the crime of "identity theft" has skyrocketed in the United States. Even if the perpetrator is caught, a person's credit may be ruined for years and the person victimized may end up having to pay thousands of dollars to rectify the matter.

Recently the U.S. Supreme Court ruled "victims of identity theft or other credit fraud cannot stretch a two-year deadline to sue companies that collect or spread bad information, even if the victims don't learn of the problem until it's too late." This case involved a California woman's identity that had been stolen by a receptionist in her doctor's office. The receptionist stole and used the woman's private personal information to apply for credit and abused it. The victimized woman sued a credit-reporting agency for failing in its responsibility to identify this problem for her. Later, when the woman asked the credit reporting agency to delete the fraudulent information it complied. However, the damage already had been done.

The Court said it was too late, when the woman sued, because she had allowed the two-year time limit to elapse. Therefore, the Court said, in essence, "too bad!" **That's why you need to know what's in your credit report and you need to know as soon as possible. As soon as you find any errors or mistakes, correct them!**

Affirmation for Wealth

I am in a wealthy place!
I give tithes and offerings to God's servants and ministries that are
feeding my spirit.
For LORD you said that whoever gives your disciples one cup of water to
drink in your name, you will give them a great reward.
I claim my reward of wealth and prosperity today.
In the name of Jesus Christ, I will never be broke another day in my life.
I am anointed with the wealth favor of God-NOW!

Chapter Eleven

STEWARDSHIP

The 90% Rule teaches that the foundation for wealth and prosperity for a believer is stewardship. In essence, stewardship means that all Christians have a financial responsibility to God – tithes and offerings. I often would wonder why there are so many broke and bankrupt Christians until I read John Avanzini's book, WAR ON DEBT – Breaking the Power of Debt. In it he made a statement so profoundly shocking that it knocked my socks off! "The average Christian spends only $2.17 per week on all Christian-related items." This includes tithes, offerings, pledges, books, tapes and conferences.

> **"The average Christian spends only $2.17 per week on all Christian-related items."**
> **John Avanzini**

Now I know why the church has so little resources for missions and assistance to the poor. **The 90% Rule** informs us, in order to receive, a Christian must first give. Not only must a Christian give, we must be "cheerful" givers (Galatians 6:7-10). If you want a financial blessing, you must make a financial offering. The basic stinginess by Christians is, in large part, why there are so many with severe financial problems.

Will a man rob God? Yet ye have robbed me. But ye say, wherein have we robbed thee? In tithes and offerings. Ye are cursed with a curse: for ye have robbed me, even this whole nation.

Bring ye all the tithes into the storehouse, that there may be meat in mine house, and prove me now herewith, saith the LORD of hosts, if I will not open you the windows of heaven, and pour you out a blessing, that there shall not be room enough to receive it (Malachi 3:8-10).

Robbing God financially is in large measure why so many people are cursed financially, particularly Christians. It is not a matter of fairness; it is because of ignorance that most people are broke, frustrated and bankrupt. In essence, if you make no deposit, you get no return. For a financial blessing, we are required to make a financial offering to God. It is our reasonable service to pay God, just as we pay our secular creditors.

Ladies and gentlemen, you do not have to take my word for it. God has already spoken. Even though I am living proof that **The 90% Rule** works and will work for you, God has given you proof. This is the only place in the Bible (Malachi 3:10) where we can test God. If we apply **The 90% Rule** to our lives, God will grant us a financial blessing we will not have room enough to receive. In essence, it's an overflow blessing of total life prosperity. The 10% you pay to your church (place of worship) represents your tithe, which is required by God. Try God and see for yourself!

The Tithe

At the 1999 International Covenant Ministries' Minister's Conference, John Avanzini unveiled a new book, STEWARD Tips. The primary goal of STEWARD Tips is the same as **The 90% Rule,** to take you to a wealthy place. In our holy journey to this wealthy place, we learned as Abraham, we are required to tithe. Tithing simply means that we must give God 10% of our earnings.

Also, like Abraham, when we are obedient and fully committed to God, He will give us wealth.

The first thing Abraham did with his great wealth was to give a tithe to God (Genesis 14:20). That's why in **The 90% Rule**'s Sample Budget the first line item is for the tithe. As the seed of Abraham and heirs of the promise, we must do the same thing. As God has moved upon my spirit and in my heart, I wish above all else that you were anointed ("empowered to prosper") – in your life, health, family, profession and in your walk with God. Remember, through the anointing of **The 90% Rule**, my goal is to get money to you.

Remember, through the anointing of The 90% Rule, my goal is to get money to you.

God has placed great emphasis on the tithe. God also has placed great promises with His emphasis on tithing (Malachi 3:8-12). Not only will you be destitute financially, you will be cursed in all that you are for not tithing. It's not the amount of the tithe that's important it's the obedience to God's Word on tithing that's important. When you follow God's Word on tithing, He will shower you with overflowing blessings of wealth.

STEWARD Tips expanded my awareness and confirmed my mission as to why it's so important for Christians to tithe – the tithe is holy. Mr. Avanzini tells us that, "If the tithe is holy to God, it should also be holy to His Children" (Leviticus 27:30). God wants you to be financially blessed (Proverbs 10:22). When the children of God are not walking in financial abundance, it impacts on world evangelism (Romans 10:13). While salvation is free

(Lord's death on Calvary), there is a cost for delivering the Gospel to mankind. Someone has to pay this significant expense (Romans 10:15; Matthew 28:19-20). It takes money to get books printed, to host workshops and conferences, to get the message of God on television and radio and to take the Gospel of Jesus Christ worldwide.

> **"If the tithe is holy to God, it should also be holy to His Children."**
> **John Avanzini**

Mr. Avanzini continued in STEWARD Tips not only to explain the importance of tithes and offerings, but he also told us why the body of Christ must be debt-free. One of the most sobering realizations in God's way of evangelizing the world for a believer is that **it takes financial resources to reach the world**. "Most people will do the praising, dancing and shouting, but it's up to the true believer to gather up the money for their time of feasting." Without a doubt, this is the real reason believers are so aptly referred to as co-laborers with Jesus (1Corinthians 3:9).

> **"The tithe is required, the offering is a voluntary gift."**
> **John Avanzini**

The Offering

As for the offering God's people give, Mr. Avanzini interjected this point in STEWARD Tips: "**The tithe is required, the offering is a voluntary gift**." Practicing the techniques of **The 90% Rule** will help you to bring God His tithe and give your offering. Mr. Avanzini stated

> **"If you have a financial need then plant a financial seed."**
> **Creflo A. Dollar, Jr.**

clearly: "It goes without saying that money from the offering always comes as a great blessing to the house of God. However, contrary to common belief, the main purpose for the offering is not to bless God's house. Its greatest purpose is to get finances to God's children." I didn't know this, otherwise I would have cleaned up my financial act earlier. God looks upon the offerings of His children as seeds they have planted for a harvest.

The giving of an offering is a discretionary action, wholly dependent on the free will of the donor (2 Corinthians 9:6-7). I think Dr. Creflo A. Dollar, Jr., said it best: "If you have a financial need, then plant a financial seed." God considers it a personal robbery when one of His children refuses to tithe or give offerings (Malachi 3:8). The reason for God's concern is that when there is no SEED PLANTED, we rob God of one of the greatest personal pleasures He has set aside for Himself, the pleasure He gets from blessing His servants.

Barbara Martin showed, in her book Minimum Wage to Maximum Wealth, how we should look at our personal life as it relates to finances. These are practical examples that, through **The 90% Rule** and prayer, have made a big change in how I look at my income.

Your Personal Life

1. **Look objectively at what is stealing every penny you earn.**

2. **Nobody is holding you back except you.** *Be your own best friend instead of your own worst enemy.*
3. **Stop being a poor person and open a savings account.**
4. **After you've figured out how much you can *realistically* save each payday, set some financial goals *and* stick to *them.***
5. **Start educating yourself about money.**
6. **Start talking money to co-workers and friends who might become the nucleus of a support group.** *But a word of caution: Because the last thing you need is to be laughed at or discouraged, don't tell them the details of what you're planning or doing unless they show a sincere interest in doing the same.*
7. **Start talking with financial planners.**
8. **Examine critically and talk back to advertising of all kinds and let those messages know *you absolutely positively will no longer respond to Pavlovian manipulation or emotional appeals that insult your intelligence.*** When you can develop that degree of smarts, then you'll buy what *you* need and want and *only* when you want it.
9. **Be prepared to backslide. By backsliding I mean there will be times you will be *very* tempted to throw in the towel.** Resist the *temptation, brothers and sisters*! Amen?
   Amen indeed!

Think long and hard before you allow your future prosperity to go down the drain. If you have blown it with your finances, start where you are today and turn your life around using **The 90% Rule**. Because there's good news with **The 90% Rule,** you are a winner. Winners pick themselves up and start again – as often as it takes.

My high school football coach (Charlie Jennett) used to tell us daily that "winners never quit and quitters never win." Even in a driving rainstorm, and we were behind by four touchdowns, we never gave up because we believed we were winners. I'm here to tell you today, child of God, that **you are a winner!** You are a winner whose determination and perseverance (the Bible calls it faith) will get you where you are going. Where you are going is into a land of wealth and prosperity.

How can I say that with **The 90% Rule** you're a winner and you're headed to a land of wealth and prosperity? Let me answer your question with a question that God asked Abraham. "*Is anything too hard for God*?" (Genesis 18:14). If God has the power to step out in the midst of nothingness and create the world and all that's within it, surely He has the power to bless you (empower you to prosper) with wealth and prosperity. His Son and our Savior Jesus Christ has long since freed us from economic bondage and granted us the petitions of our hearts (Mark 11:23-24). We just have to believe it and accept it. He reminds us of the promise God made to us at the dawning of time.

We're All in This Together

In a recent national survey, more than 80 percent of Americans consider themselves Christians. Although our population has immigration from Europe, Africa, the Caribbean, the Far East and Arab world, our population has grown and new religions have barely dented the overwhelmingly Christian composition of the U.S. population. This was the finding from a 13-month survey of 113,000 adults. Study Director Barry Kosmin of the City University of New York Graduate School called the findings the most extensive religious profile available of 20th-century America.

The survey found 86.5% of Americans identified with Christian Denominations, including 26% Roman Catholic and 60% Protestant.

The survey found 86.5% of Americans identified with Christian denominations, including 26 percent Roman Catholic and 60 percent Protestant. Only 2 percent refused to reveal their religious identification, and only 7.5 percent said they had no religion. If 86.5 percent of the United States' population is Christian, then we have a lot of broke, bankrupt and financially distraught Christians.

There is one common thread running through all these different religious groups – economic bondage. **The 90% Rule** is a non-denominational truth that will benefit all who apply it. **The 90% Rule** is your ticket to economic freedom.

Three Things We Must Know

For more than 30 years, Kenneth Copeland has been preaching the ministry and message of prosperity. In his book, PROSPERITY: The Choice is Yours, he tells us that the body of Christ must know three things regarding the laws of prosperity. If you are ignorant of these three things you are a problem going somewhere to happen.

1. **You must know that it is God's will to prosper His people.** God is not limited by what part of the world you live in or what government you live under.

2. **We need to know God's reason for prospering His people.** The whole purpose for gainful employment and prosperity is to take God's laws and prosper by them and then do something about the poverty in the rest of the world. God intended for material creation to bless and prosper His people.
3. **The last thing we must know is God's way of prospering His people.** God prospers by prospering the soul and through the avenue of giving.

> **"Satan, I bind you from my finances according to Matthew 18:18 and loose you from your assignment against me."**
> **Prayers That Avail Much**

Consistent with Kenneth Copeland's counsel, Deuteronomy 8:18 amplifies this point. "*But thou shalt remember the Lord thy God: for it is he that giveth thee power to get wealth, that he may establish his covenant which he sware unto thy fathers, as it is this day.*"

An Intercessory Prayer for Prosperity

The 90% Rule requires a biblical basis for all that I do regarding my finances. The Word of God has been my sword and shield as I defeated the demons of debt. The Word of God must be deeply immersed daily with prayer. In the book, Prayers That Avail Much, by WORD MINISTRIES, INC., I found an excellent intercessory prayer that I use as my prayer for prosperity.

"Father, in the name of your son, Jesus, I confess your word over me this day. As I do this, I say it with my mouth and believe it in my heart and know that your word will not return to you void, but will accomplish what it says it will do.

"Therefore, I believe in the name of Jesus that my needs are met according to Philippians 4:19. I believe that because I have given to further your cause, Father, gifts will be given to me, good measure, pressed down, shaken together and running over will they pour into my bosom. For with the measure I deal out, it will be measured back to me. Father, I confess a hundredfold return for me according to Mark 10:29-30.

"Father, you have delivered me out of the authority of darkness into the kingdom of your dear Son. Father, I believe I have taken his place as your child. I confess you have assumed your place as my Father and have made your home with me. You are taking care of me and even now enabling me to walk in love and in wisdom, and to walk in the fullness of fellowship with your Son.

"SATAN, I BIND YOU FROM MY FINANCES ACCORDING TO MATTHEW 18:18 AND LOOSE YOU FROM YOUR ASSIGNMENT AGAINST ME.

"I thank you that the ministering spirits which you have given to me are now free to minister for me and bring in the necessary finances.

"Father, I confess you are a very present help in trouble, and you are more than enough. I confess, God, you are able to make all grace, every favor and earthly blessing, come to me in abundance, so that I am always in all circumstances and whatever the need, self-sufficient, possessing enough to require no aid or support and furnished in abundance for every good work and charitable donation."

Affirmation for Wealth

I am in a wealthy place!
I pray daily.
I remember that God has promised me long life and peace.
I trust in the LORD with all my heart and lean not on
my own understanding.
In the name of Jesus Christ, I will never be broke another day in my life!
I am anointed with the wealth favor of God-NOW!

Chapter Twelve

PRACTICING PROSPERITY

Clipping Coupons

In addition to giving you what the Bible says will help you gain wealth and prosperity, **The 90% Rule** also gives you some common sense information that has blessed my family. Remember in Chapter Seven, where Paul Richard told us "Nearly 32 cents out of every dollar American families spend is for groceries and household items"? Well, here's a common sense way we save money on nearly a third of ever dollar we spend: clipping coupons.

> **By clipping coupons you can save, on average, between 20% and 50% on the cost of groceries.**

By clipping coupons, you can save, on average, between 20% and 50% on the cost of groceries. This is a great low-cost way to save hundreds of dollars but you will have to put forth some effort. The first step is obtaining the coupons: Most major newspapers offer a goldmine of coupons in their Sunday editions. Some papers also offer coupons in the grocery edition. In our hometown, the grocery editions are published on Wednesdays and Thursdays, and they offer a plethora of grocery bargains and coupons. You also can pick up coupons in the grocery stores themselves. These stores usually have their own "sales paper," which lists in-store coupons and special discounts.

The key thing to remember about coupons is that you should collect only those you're going to use. Therefore, look to your specific family's grocery list (see ours in Chapter Seven). Look for the coupons and specials on the specific goods and brands that your family uses. Another treasure trove of coupons can be found from local high school community organizations. As band parents for more than 10 years, we sold hundreds of coupon books to individuals as fundraisers. Of course, we used less than 10% of the coupons in the book. The use of specifically targeted coupons has allowed us to save at least 35% on our groceries. You can also combine your coupons with manufacturers' coupons and discounts on the actual products themselves.

Another source of coupons is the actual grocery receipt from the register. Occasionally, I have found some useful coupons on the register receipts. In addition to coupons for groceries, most major service providers and manufacturers offer coupons. We use coupons for discounted service on our cars (oil changes, tune ups, etc.), our home (carpet cleaners, free check of the heating/cooling system), communications (telephone, cable, satellite, etc.), laundry/dry cleaning and vacations. Again, you just have to check out the type of coupons, the terms and conditions for the coupons, to ensure they are worthwhile and will be used.

The 90% Rule's key to coupon clipping is to collect only those coupons you know you will use.

The 90% Rule's key to coupon clipping is to collect only those coupons you know you will use.

Anything else is just clutter. Remember, you have a specific grocery list that is only for your family. Therefore, collect only the coupons for the brands that your family appreciates. For other coupon savings, keep this strategy in mind. If there's a $19.95 brake special for Toyotas and you own a Buick, this is not the coupon you should consider.

Incidentals

The 90% Rule has reduced our overall costs of non-food items to 42%. Speaking of toiletries, store brands are usually less expensive than nationally advertised brands. I do not purchase any brands unless they are on sale. Some of you may say, "What if I run out before they go on sale?" I do not run out because I buy in volume. Most of the sales on toiletries are either two-for-one or a price so reduced that multiple purchases may be made. Remember, you are buying for at least two months.

> **Another way to "get more bang for your (toiletries) buck" is to use common sense. Toothpaste should be squeezed from the bottom to the top, which will ensure that practically every drop will be used.**

Another way to "get more bang for your (toiletries) buck" is to use common sense. Toothpaste should be squeezed from the bottom to the top, which will ensure that practically every drop will be used. Lotion and deodorant containers may be turned upside down, after use, to ensure all of the product will be used. If you throw away one ounce of lotion or deodorant a month, you will have lost the equivalent of three bottles by the end of the year – "Waste not, want not." Additionally, from my travel, I have received numerous complimentary toiletries (soap, shampoo, and conditioner) from hotels, as freebies.

Dress For Success

After I left the temporary government job, I re-opened my legal practice. **The 90% Rule** allowed me to dress for success. As a lawyer, I am required to wear a suit and tie during the week. As a minister, I also wear the same attire on the weekend. How do I keep a contemporary wardrobe? First, I wear quality conservative style suits because they are always in style. I also wear conservative colors (blue, gray, brown, black, green). Normally, I will drive my family to a different outlet mall every six months or so to shop. By careful inspection, we have found some tremendous bargains on clothing for our entire family.

The suits may not have current styling, however, they can be purchased for as little as $20. A tailor or seamstress can perform minor alterations (lapel tapered, waist/length altered) for $25. Therefore, a quality suit can be had for less than $50, including alterations.

When necessary, I purchase shirts and ties, unless I need to add a pair of slacks. When I purchase at department stores, I always buy suits from the clearance rack. For example, the premium suits at major retailers (Sears, J C Penney, etc.) that normally sell for $250 to $500 can be bought for $89 to $100 off the clearance rack. A new 100% silk tie will compliment these suits as to style and quality. Also, buy quality leather shoes and have them re-soled when needed. I have a 15-year-old pair that still looks good after five re-soles.

Another good place to purchase suits is thrift stores (i.e., Goodwill, Salvation Army, etc.). Remember to be very careful and check these clothes thoroughly. The suits may not have current styling; however, they can be purchased for as little as $20. A tailor or seamstress can perform minor alterations (lapel tapered, waist/length altered) for $25. Therefore, a quality suit can be had for less than $50, including alterations. When buying from a thrift store, always stick with basic colors and basic styles. Make sure you dry clean (or otherwise clean) all garments before wearing them. Once again, a quality contemporary tie can do wonders for the suit.

Although I talked primarily about men's attire, women can do even better at the outlet malls, on the clearance racks of department stores and at thrift stores. There are so many more stores and shops offering women's clothing. Also, a scarf, bag, shoes or shawl can beautifully accent their outfits. There are also flea markets all over the country selling new, almost new and used clothing, hardware, appliances and other products at substantial discounts. Remember, shop around and compare. It has worked for my family and our clothing costs have been reduced by at least 30% to 50%.

The 90% Rule allows you to spend less for your "Gotta Pays" and "Must Haves," leaving you more to spend on debt reduction and savings.

Little Things

Good grooming is extremely important, yet expensive. For me to get a haircut with wash and conditioner is $25. The haircut alone is $10. I had been getting my hair cut at least twice a month and sometimes more often. There was also a one-and-a-half- to two-hour wait for service.

I wear a very conservative hair cut, which is easy to cut and maintain. Therefore, for $29.99, I bought a complete barber's kit (clippers, attachments, combs, and scissors). I have been cutting my own hair for about five years and this barber kit has paid for itself, hundreds of times over. Additionally, I do it in the privacy of my own home at a time that is convenient to me, saving untold hours of time. If you cannot serve as your own barber, shop around and save.

For my wife and daughters, trips to the hair salon are a lot more expensive, averaging about $75 each (perms, conditioner, styling, etc.) and their trips are more frequent, usually every other week. Sometimes they will do their own hair to save money. These costs may be reduced; however, good grooming is necessary for the entire family.

Although **The 90% Rule** provides you a lifestyle with the most efficient use of your finances (tithing, savings, investing) you don't have to give up your quality of life. I recognize there are some things you are required to pay in order to live and some things you must have to fully appreciate your self worth. "Gotta Pays" are necessities like your tithes, rent or mortgage, utilities, groceries, etc. "Must Haves" are personals like clothing, toiletries, grooming and other personal hygiene items.

The 90% Rule allows you to spend less for your Gotta Pays and Must Haves, leaving you more to spend on debt reduction and savings. It does not matter how much money you earn, what matters is how much of your earnings you are able to keep. Every now and then, take your family out to dinner or a movie from the funds you set aside (in your budget) for entertainment. We have been able to save money on each purchase by using **The 90% Rule**.

Major savings for food and perishables are also available by joining buying clubs (e.g., Sam's, etc.). You also can save a bundle by volume purchases. When buying in bulk, make sure you have adequate storage (freezer, cabinet, etc.) before buying. You don't want to buy more just to have more waste – "waste not want not".

Welcome Home

The 90% Rule recognizes that most people in the United States' primary source of wealth is in their homes. **The 90% Rule**'s common sense of practicality greatly

Initially, we had a $50,000 adjustable rate mortgage, which we wrapped the down payment into a renovation loan (a 90-day balloon payment). Therefore, the actual out-of-pocket fund at closing was $30.10.

benefited us in becoming homeowners. We rented our (condominium) home for two-and-a-half years before we purchased it. It was 13 years old, in a great neighborhood with higher priced homes than ours and needed some work. The appraised value was $62,500, in need of about $5,000 worth of repairs – mostly cosmetic (painting, replacing trim), upgrading plumbing fixtures and a new garbage disposal. We were able to purchase it for $55,000, with a 10% down payment. Initially, we had a $50,000 adjustable rate mortgage and we wrapped the down payment into a renovation loan (a 90-day balloon payment). Therefore, the actual out-of-pocket fund at closing was $30.10.

The common sense of **The 90% Rule** also led us to make repairs (doing the work we were qualified to do ourselves) rather than purchase replacements wherever practical. With assistance from the home improvement store and some part time help, I was able to perform the minor repairs (painting, lighting fixtures, doorbell, patio, shrubbery trimming) and saved more than $2,000.

After several searches, I was able to find a heating and cooling specialist who performed a complete system check and upgrade of our central heat/air conditioning for $1,000. I also found a plumber who performed the necessary plumbing system repairs for $2,000. Afterwards, the value increased to $75,000, with only a $50,000 mortgage. This gave us an immediate $25,000 equity in our home.

When the interest rates went down in 2001, we refinanced our condominium. By then our value had risen to $89,000 and our daughters were in college. We refinanced with a lower rate, saving nearly $100 per month on payments and more than $140,000 in total interest payments. More importantly, we pulled $20,000 out of our equity (now we have a $60,000 mortgage) to pay the girls' tuition and some credit card debt. We still have $29,000 in equity, $5,000 more than we had originally. Home ownership is the best universal way to gain wealth in the United States.

Car Wars

In June of 1990, I sold my 1989 Porsche 944 to my former law partner for the remaining payments. I was not trying to make a profit; I was trying to liquidate a $735 per month (for six years) obligation. This was a tremendous burden lifted, since I had two other cars and two other notes. Remember, it's not how much you make, it's how much of your earnings you keep. A major component of **The 90% Rule** is reducing your expenses, which results in increasing your income.

Three years later, June 1993, I sold my 1990 Nissan Maxima to my former secretary, also for the remaining payments. This saved me $311.32 per month for the remaining 36 months. I originally had a five-year note (at $611.50 per month) on this car. I had earlier refinanced it to lower my payments.

I was able to sell this car based on unusual circumstances. My ex-wife blew the engine in her 1988 Isuzu Imark. I took her to the Subaru dealership and negotiated a great deal for her on a new car. She then sold me her broken down Isuzu for $250. I had to have it towed 25 miles to the Isuzu dealer for repairs. I used my AAA membership to get the car towed for free, saving at least $100. This was a great deal, considering my AAA membership is only $50 per year.

For over two and a half years I had worry free transportation. Total cost $1,147 and no payments (costs about five cents a mile). During that time I put 24,000 miles on the car, with only regular oil changes and tune ups.

I had the engine repaired to run

and other necessary mechanical systems repaired for $897. The radio, inside dome lights and inside trunk release latch did not work. I did not need these things; I needed transportation. For over two-and-a-half years, I had worry-free transportation. The total cost was $1,147 and no payments (costs about five cents a mile). During that time, I put 24,000 miles on the car, with only regular oil changes and tune ups. If you compare the refinanced payments on the Maxima and add it to the Porsche payments, I saved $1,046.32 per month for 30 months (a total savings of $31,389.60). One monthly payment is only $99.68 less than the total amount paid for the Isuzu.

Energy Efficiency

To save money on utilities, there are a number of actions we have taken. Cooking after dinner during non-peak hours, with open kitchen windows for ventilation and cooling is a cheaper, more efficient use of electricity. Non-peak hours' usage of electricity is cheaper than when everyone else is using it. Keeping the thermostat at 70 degrees (Summer and Winter) lessens the strain on the central heating and cooling unit. The heating/air conditioning system works more efficiently at one constant temperature. In Florida, with the 90-degree plus temperatures (three-fourths of the year) 70 degrees is also quite comfortable.

Always, turn off lights when leaving the room. Get what you want out of the refrigerator and close the door! Change your heating/cooling system's filter at least three times a year. You can

Keeping the thermostat at 70 degrees (Summer and Winter) lessens the strain on the central heating and cooling unit. Always, turn off lights when leaving the room. Get what you want out of the refrigerator and close the door!

pur-chase these filters for as little as $3 to $7 dollars each. These few dollars can save you hundreds of dollars over the year by enhancing your system's efficiency.

Throughout **The 90% Rule**, I have given you various scriptures – pertaining to debt freedom, prosperity living and practical activities – that you can place in your ears as a faith seed. Keep these words before your eyes – read them daily. Keep them in your ears – say them to yourself and others, as affirmations. And keep them before your mouth – read them aloud.

My calling, experience and knowledge provided the system for The 90% Rule, but it is God who will grant you the increase (1 Corinthians 3:6).

Affirmation for Wealth

I am in a wealthy place!
I pray daily.
I am a child of the Most High God.
I remember the promise of God to me, that He will give me
the desires of my heart.
I remember that I can do all things through Christ Jesus.
I remember that Jesus Christ came that I may have a more abundant life.
In the name of Jesus Christ, I will never be broke another day in my life.
I am anointed with the wealth favor of God-NOW!

Chapter Thirteen

IN A WEALTHY PLACE

Brothers and sisters, **The 90% Rule** is a "**textbook for tithers**" and its sole purpose is to take you to a wealthy place. Throughout **The 90% Rule**, you also have been exposed to the spiritual and practical aspects of maintaining your standard of living while getting out of debt and obtaining wealth and prosperity. Child of God, if you have missed everything I have told you to this point, don't miss this point: **God will hold you accountable for all that He has blessed you with**. *For unto whomsoever much is given, of him shall be much required*" (Luke 14:48).

The 90% Rule is a "textbook for tithers."

Learn from the wisdom of God concerning your wealth and prosperity. In the parable of the talents in Matthew 25:14-30, Jesus lets you know that life is about choices – which will you follow and how will you conduct yourself? God has blessed each of us with a certain amount of time, talent and tribute. What matters most is not what God has given to us, what matters is what we do with the time, talent and tribute God has entrusted in our care. Are you a good and faithful servant, or a wicked and slothful servant? Only you can answer this question truthfully.

If you are a born again believer in Jesus Christ, you are not a "wicked and slothful servant." You are a believer in the son of the living God who has come that you may have a more abundant life. I also believe that if you follow the spiritual and practical principles laid out in **The 90% Rule**, you will do great things to the glory of God. There's nothing greater that you can do than to make maximum use of the time, talent and tribute that God has blessed you with. Because, when you do, then in your finances, family, health and service to God, you will live a truly blessed life. Such that God will say to you: *Well done, good and faithful servant; thou hast been faithful over a few things, I will make thee ruler over many things: enter thou into the joy of thy lord* (Matthew 25:23).

The 90% Rule is my ministry with a mission: to teach you the truth about God's will for you. This book is also a cry from my soul as an appeal to you to come to Jesus. To do otherwise is too terrible for me to contemplate. If you are not a born again believer in Jesus Christ, and if you do not take care of what God has given you, He will take everything away from you – money, health, companionship, etc. – and give it all to someone who already has more. There is no quality of life when you're poor, broke and hungry.

There is no quality of life when you're poor, broke and hungry.

A hungry person does not care about salvation; he or she is just looking for food. A bankrupt person does not care about the resurrection; he or she is just looking for money to make ends meet. A poor person is not interested in the Trinity; he or she is just looking for a better life. Additionally, a person who is poor, broke and hungry will not give to God or anyone else. **The 90% Rule** provides you with the necessary tools to manage the financial talents God has given you that will bring you good success.

The 90% Rule also provides a vehicle for church leaders to empower believers with the necessary financial resources to meet their obligations to God and to their families. Therefore, believers will have no reason to rob God of His tithes and offerings. Believers will have no reason to have to choose between giving to God and providing for their families. Jesus Christ came into the world as Lord and Savior to give us a "more" abundant life (John 10:10). The question a lot of believers have is how I can live this "more abundant life." The answer is **The 90% Rule**!

The 90% Rule provides you with the necessary tools to manage the financial talents God has given you that will bring you good success.

The 90% Rule provides a way out for you, just like God provided a "ram in the bush" for Abraham. Just look to the Word of God and you can become free from the bondage of debt. *Let them shout for joy, and be glad, that favor my righteous cause: yea, let them say continually, let the Lord be magnified, which hath pleasure in the prosperity of his servant* (Psalm 35:27). You must remember to keep first things first: worship God in spirit and truth, bring your tithes and offerings into His storehouse and seek God's kingdom and righteousness; then all of your needs will be met.

The 90% Rule also will equip you to handle your current finances and it will provide you with a system of operation that will absolutely get you out of debt. We are required to meditate on the Word of God day and night and continually say out loud our affirmations of prosperity (Joshua 1:8). If you follow **The 90% Rule**, you will get out of debt, you will know how to manage your resources, you will know the proper order of things (put God first) and you will become a living testimony that the system works. Now, you are ready for the ultimate, you are ready for a supernatural financial blessing. You are ready to go to a wealthy place!

As you have seen through my life and Job and his life, God has great things in store for those who love him. Before I could come into a wealthy place, I had to learn to stop wasting God's resources. Now that I know, through **The 90% Rule**, I want to tell everyone who will listen that Jesus is both Lord and Savior. My beginning was small and, because of my lack of knowledge, I squandered it. But because of Jesus' grace and mercy, my latter end has increased abundantly (Job 8:7). God loves you so much that he wants to give you the desires of your heart. **The 90% Rule** allows you to come and go with me to a wealthy place.

After all that I have been through (money, lack of knowledge, bankruptcy, wealth), I now know what Paul meant when he said: "*And we know that all things work together for good to them that love God, to them that are the called according to His purpose*" (Romans 8:28). Through listening to God, prayer, fasting, meditation on His Word and stepping out on faith, **The 90% Rule** brought all things together for me.

Deuteronomy 8:1 **(The Prime Directive; Genesis 1:28)**

Deuteronomy 8:2-4 **(Remember what God has already done for you)**
Deuteronomy 8:5-6 **(Think before you act)**
Deuteronomy 8:7-9 **(A Wealthy Place)**
Deuteronomy 8:10 **(Give Praise and Thanks to the LORD)**
Deuteronomy 8:11-16 **(God's testimony in your life)**
Deuteronomy 8:17 **(Your ego can destroy you)**
Deuteronomy 8:18 **(The Promise of God)**

When all things work together for your good, you will have all of your personal needs (food, clothing, shelter, wealth, good health, etc.) met. It is not God's wish that any (believer) should perish, rather, he wants you to live long and prosper (2 Peter 3:9)!

The Prime Directive

Some of you may be wondering if you, or any Christian, deserves to prosper in life. Let me help remove all doubt from your mind right now. Don't let yourself or anyone else talk you out of your blessing from God. The first thing God did after creating Adam and Eve was to anoint them. He blessed them, anointed them to prosper in life. Then God blessed them with perfect health, wealth and prosperity and the authority to serve as stewards (trustees) of the earth. "*Be fruitful and multiply and replenish the earth, and subdue it*" (Genesis 1:28). I call this passage of Scripture, "**The Prime Directive**."

The "Prime Directive" of **The 90% Rule** is the guiding principle for man's existence on this planet. To be fruitful means that you are blessed with manifold blessings in life, health, wealth, goodness, peace, love, joy and all of the fruits of the Spirit. God gave Adam and Eve the Prime

Directive before allowing them to set out on their journey (have dominion over the earth). As Christians, God also gives us the same "Prime Directive." To disobey God's "Prime Directive" (disobedience through sin) brings about death. To obey the "Prime Directive" allows us to receive the gift of God through Jesus Christ (Romans 6:23).

God's "Prime Directive" tells me that we have been empowered to prosper in every aspect of our lives. He blessed us. He anointed us to be fruitful and multiply. He told us to subdue the earth and have dominion over its habitants. Therefore, we are to have dominion over our resources – time, talents, tribute – and dominion over our words, actions and thoughts. In this directive, we have been given all we need to prosper. Through sin (Satan) a "poor, broke and hungry" mentality has infected the lives of many believers. This mentality has taken the children of God away from their rightful place on earth.

Brothers and sisters, we are more than conquerors through Christ Jesus who strengthens us (Philippians 4:13). You have got to get away from these old traditions (i.e., "pie in the sky, bye and bye," "I'll just wait until my chance comes", etc.) and go to a new land where God Almighty is leading you.

I have personally used The 90% Rule to get wealth.

If you read Genesis Chapters 12 through 17, you will see how God blessed Abraham financially. In fact, God blessed Abraham and all that he touched. His nephew Lot got rich just by hanging around Abraham. This is a fundamental principle: **wealth attracts other wealth**.

The 90% Rule is a new way of thinking for Christians. It is not a new message. It is a realization that God still wants us to be blessed. Jesus said, "I am the way, the truth, and the life" (John 14:6). **The 90% Rule** is a spiritual revelation of a simple truth: with God all things are possible (Matthew 19:26).

I have personally used **The 90% Rule** to get wealth and I thank and praise God for His many blessings. It will also help you get your heart right, because it is God who gives us the power to get wealth. For as many of us that believe, Jesus has given us the power (authority) to become the sons and daughters of God (John 1:12). Now you know, with **The 90% Rule**, that God wants you to be in perfect health and blessed with great prosperity. You need to know this so that you can be like Abraham. When you obtain wealth, you can say no man made me wealthy, it was God (Genesis 14:23).

Bless the LORD with Tithes and Offerings

As a child of God, when you fail to tithe and give offerings, you literally block your own bountiful blessings. This is the formula that God set out for us centuries ago (Malachi 3:10). That means that after you have finished praying, fasting and reading **The 90% Rule**, you've got to get up and act on it in order to receive the necessary resource to meet your obligation to God and your family (James 1:22). As I have systematically educated and motivated you with **The 90% Rule**, to tithe and give offerings, I have positioned you for receiving financial blessings from the Lord. Not only that,

The 90% Rule is God's vision for His children to live free from debt and for a life of wealth and prosperity.

but I also have helped you bring pleasure to God as He blesses you.

The 90% Rule is God's truth on living debt-free and in full prosperity! As we begin to understand the purpose and principles of sowing and reaping, giving to God will cease to be drudgery, and there will be more than enough in our houses, as well as in God's house. After five years of living, practicing, praying and believing the anointing of **The 90% Rule,** God has blessed me like He blessed Job. Just like Job, the LORD gave me back everything doubled! (Job 42:12-16).

What Have We Learned?

We have learned that **The 90% Rule** is God's vision for His children to live free from debt and for a life of wealth and prosperity. Throughout **The 90% Rule**, I have provided you a list of daily personal affirmations for you **to read, meditate on and say aloud and add to your daily schedule of prayer and devotion**.

Affirmation for Wealth

I am in a wealthy place!
I speak aloud my affirmations of wealth and prosperity daily.
I "call those things that be not as though they were".
I remember that whosever shall call upon the name of the LORD shall
be saved.
In the name of Jesus Christ, I will never be broke another day in my life.
I am anointed with the wealth favor of God-NOW!

Chapter Fourteen

QUESTIONS AND ANSWERS

Wisdom is the principal thing:
Therefore get wisdom: and with
All thy getting get understanding.
(Proverbs 4:7)

After having gone through the many ups and downs of the last 17 years – from turmoil in life to trust in God – I am anointed with the wealth of God. Some of you may wonder, how is this possible? As I travel the country teaching **The 90% Rule,** people ask me some interesting questions including, "Why did it take so long?" One of the most profound questions was when did everything come together for me.

The purpose of Chapter Fourteen is to explain to Christian believers that unless we obtain the wisdom of God, through gaining an understanding of His Word, we are doomed to failure. My father preached the Gospel for more than 58 years, my brother has preached for more than 20 years, my late brother-in-law preached for more than 60 years and I have preached for more than 15 years. However, it has been only within the last five years that I have been able to preach with the power and wisdom of God. If you're preaching and no lives are being blessed in your congregation, then you need to change your message. When your preaching and teaching is under-girded with prayer, then souls will be saved, lives will be changed and the body of Christ will be blessed.

When did everything fall into place for you and how did you know it had happened?

It was in 1997 when I actually hit rock bottom in my life. It was also the year that I experienced a true epiphany with the Holy Spirit in my life regarding my call into ministry with a mission.

A certain man had two sons
And the younger of them said to his father, Father, give me the portion of goods that falleth to me. And he divided unto them his living.
And not many days after the younger son gathered all together, and took his journey into a far country, and there wasted his substance with riotous living.
And when he had spent all, there arose a mighty famine in that land;
and he began to be in want.
And he went and joined himself to a citizen of that country; and he sent him into his fields to feed swine.
And he would fain have filled his belly with the husks the swine did eat: and no man gave unto him.
And when came to himself, he said, how many hired servants of my father's have bread enough and to spare, and I perish with hunger!
I will arise and go to my father, and will say unto him, Father, I have sinned against heaven, and before thee,
And am no more worthy to be called thy son: make me as one of thy hired servants.
And he arose, and came to his father, but when he was yet a great way off, his father saw him, and had

compassion, and ran and fell on his neck and kissed him.
And the son said unto him, Father, I have sinned against heaven, and in thy sight, and am no more worthy to be called thy son.
But the father said unto his servants, bring forth the best robe, and put it on him; and put a ring on his hand and shoes on his feet:
And bring hither the fatted calf, and kill it; and let us eat and be merry:
For this my son was dead, and is alive again; he was lost, and is found. And they began to be merry.
(Luke 15:11-24)

I have been in the pigpen. I know now what the prodigal son felt like. The prodigal son and I had lots of friends when we had "big money." But when the money dried up, our friends ran for cover and we began to be in want.

After all the pain, confusion, depression, poverty, fear and emptiness of spirit in my life, there came a knock at midnight. It was late at night and the next morning I was going to have to tell my daughters there is no future for us, only the darkness. I had cried my tear ducts dry and my throat was hoarse from calling on Jesus. At my darkest hour, my lowest moment in life, I received a call from my first wife's mother.

She called me to say that she was thinking about her granddaughters and me. She said, "I don't think of you as my son-in-law, but as my son." She said she loved me just as much as if she had birthed me herself. She told me that I was a great father to her granddaughters and she asked me if I knew how much her daughter, Rita, really loved me. I said yes and that I still loved her. She reminded me of just how important I was to her and to Jesus Christ.

As she shared her blessed love and compassion for me, I began to hear the words of "Blessed Assurance" stir in my soul.

Blessed assurance, Jesus is mine!
O what a foretaste of glory divine!
Heir of salvation, purchase of God,
Born of His Spirit, washed in his blood.
This is my story, this is my song,
Praising my savior all the day long;
This is my story, this is my song,
Praising my savior all the day long.

When she said that, she brought me back to remembrance of my grandma.

It was a wonderful feeling to reminisce and relive the magical moments of life with my grandma. It was my grandma who raised me. She was there when I gave my life to Jesus Christ at age 12. She was there to nurse me back to health after the doctors had given up on me. At age 12, the doctors had given me only two weeks to live.

Grandma was also there to comfort and care for me when at age 15 my mom died. She was there to select Rita as a wife for me – an intelligent, committed, hard working and full of the Holy Ghost woman. That night I began to have my own prayer meeting and was full of joy. My grandma's favorite hymn was "A Charge To Keep". I hear those words resonate in my spirit.

A charge to keep I have, a God to glorify

Who gave His Son my soul to save, and fit it for
the sky
To serve the present age, my calling to fulfill
O may it all my powers engage, to do my master's
will
Arm me with jealous care, As in thy sight to live
And O thy Servant, Lord, prepare A strict account
to give
Help me to watch and pray, and on thyself rely
By faith assured I will obey for I shall never die.

The memories of love, joy, peace and praise that my grandma and mother-in-law stirred up inside of me brought me back to Creflo Dollar, Jr. He ends each daily message with Proverbs 4:7. "In all your getting, get understanding."

I read Proverbs 4: 7 again and things began to solidify in my mind, heart, soul and actions. The book of Proverbs is one of the few biblical books that clearly spell out its purpose. The purpose of the Book of Proverbs is twofold: (1) to impart moral discernment and discretion, and (2) to develop mental clarity and perception. **The 90% Rule** is an anointing on my life to provide spiritual and practical wisdom of God through the Holy Spirit to be a blessing to the lives of believers.

Those two women moved me back to my center – walking holy before God. They reminded me that Proverbs, as a whole, is designed both to prevent and remedy ungodly lifestyles. I stopped looking at my circumstances and started looking at my Savior. These women forced me to look at why God spared my life at age 12. Like my grandma used to say, "the Lord didn't bring me this far just to leave me."

It was those virtues that caused me to look again at the Word of God for the first time I remembered how liberating it was for me at age 12 to give my life to Jesus Christ. I also remembered the awesome experience of God's call of me into ministry with a mission. I completed my seminary studies and began to pray for wisdom to understand and explain sound doctrine.

With so many ministers and ministries out there teaching on prosperity, whom did you listen to who helped you to understand God's message for your prosperity?

I began to discern between religious tradition and God's anointing. I also began a study of other ministries that taught how God would remove every burden and destroy every yoke (Isaiah 58:6). I found anointed men and women of God who caused a true spiritual change in my life. They are: Kenneth Copland, Creflo Dollar, Kenneth Hagan, T.D. Jakes, John Avanzini, Jerry Savel, Jesse DuPlantis, Joyce Meyer, Leroy Thompson, Larry Burkett, Lewis Lampley, Eddie Long, Charles Scriven, Charles Stanley and R.B. Holmes, Jr. They all had a profound impact on my calling, study and understanding God's Word.

The year 1997 began as the lowest point in my life (lost it all and bankrupt) and it ended being the highest point in my life – the creation of Carter Ministries. Rita and I reconciled our relationship. In 1998 we remarried and began a community outreach ministry – through Carter Ministries – in our home. We bought every book, tape and CD we could afford by the giants in ministry, listed above.

We read and listened over and over, at home, in the car, everywhere. In 1999, I started going to the International Covenant Ministries Ministers Conferences in Atlanta.

Under the dynamic spiritual leadership of Dr. Creflo A. Dollar, Jr., International Covenant Ministries helped us to grow in wisdom and understanding by leaps and bounds. It's so very important to get under the leadership of the Anointed One and His Anointing!

At the 2000 International Covenant Ministries' Ministers Conference in Atlanta, I was truly blessed. I sat under the teaching of Creflo Dollar, Kenneth Copeland, T.D. Jakes, Joyce Meyer, Oral Roberts, Leroy Thompson, Benny Hinn, John Hagee, Hilton Sutton and a world-class staff of professionals (attorneys, accountants, teachers, etc.) and my life was changed again. Just when I thought I had reached the apex of ministry, they took me to a higher level. (A complete list of my reference sources is provided for you in the Bibliography in the back of this book.)

I had been talking about **The 90% Rule** all these years, but I had not written it in a book such that others may use it. These giants in the ministry were doing what I had been hoping and praying to do. In 2001, Carter Ministries officially became a Member of International Covenant Ministries. Rita and I also became vision partners with Creflo and Taffi Dollar in their ministry. After we attended the 2001 Annual International Covenant Ministries Convention in July and the anointing came down on us, we have never looked back.

How can I determine the quality of a credit-counseling agency or professional?

Before approaching a credit agency or credit counseling professional, read **The 90% Rule** to determine what you hope to accomplish (credit counseling; debt consolidation; debt reduction plan, etc.). It's also a good idea to have your written budget and income statement. Christine Dugas provides good answers to this question in her *USA Today* article entitled: "How to check out a credit-counseling agency." Her advice and counsel mirror **The 90% Rule** and, although it's common sense, a number of people fail to do it. Call your local Better Business Bureau, your state attorney general's office and your local consumer protection agencies. In Florida, consumer protection is so important that it has been merged into a Cabinet (statewide elected official) agency: the Florida Department of Agriculture and Consumer Services.

The key to Ms. Dugas' advice is to ask key questions of the debt-counseling agency before giving them your personal financial information. The key questions are:

1. How much training do counselors receive?
2. Does it belong to a trade association that sets standards for its members, such as the National Federation for Credit Counseling (NFCC) or the Association of Independent Consumer Credit Counseling Agencies (AICCA)?
3. Does the agency have an independent board of directors?
4. Does it keep client funds in a trust account, separate from its operating funds?
5. How long has it been in business in your area?
6. Is the agency accredited?
7. What types of services does it offer?
8. How long will it take to complete a debt-management program?

9. What effect will working with a counselor have on my credit rating?
10. Are agency services confidential?

She finalizes the article with a caution to "be wary of outrageous claims."

Why is it necessary to speak daily affirmations in order to receive wealth and prosperity?

Child of God, if you say it long enough and strong enough, then you shall have the desires of your heart. The power of life and death is in the tongue (Proverbs 18:21). If you believe what you're praying for and say aloud the petitions of your heart, then you shall have what you say (Mark 11:23). Let me quote two great preachers to further illuminate the answer to this question.

This is how Jesus answered this question at Mark 11:22-23. *And Jesus answering saith unto them, Have faith in God. For verily I say unto you, That whosoever shall say unto this mountain, Be thou removed, and be thou removed, and be thou cast into the sea; and shall not doubt in his heart, but shall believe that those things which he saith shall come to pass; he shall have whatsoever he saith.* When you say it (make affirmations of faith) based on the Word of God, then you shall have what you say. In essence, you can speak your blessings into existence with faith-filled words.

Dr. Leroy Thompson, in his book, Money Cometh! To the Body of Christ, answered the question this way. "*Say this, Money cometh unto me, because my Father said so. Therefore, there will be no lack for preaching the Gospel, nor in my personal affairs. I am not covetous with the Lord's blessings, but I am a covenant partner with the plan, purpose and will of God. God is my source. God is my supplier. Therefore, I will always have more than enough. Money is not my master. Jesus is my master. I master and manage my money according to the will of God. And money cometh to me! By making these kinds of confessions, you are watering the seeds of God's Word sown, and you are enabling God to bring increase into your life."*

As a young couple expecting a child, can you tell us what you think it will cost to raise a newborn baby to age six?

A recent issue of Consumer Reports provided, in my opinion, the best answer to this question.

- A couple earning $23,000 annually will spend $47,243 to raise a newborn to age six.
- A couple earning $50,600 annually will spend $65,918 to raise a newborn to age six.
- A couple earning $95,800 annually will spend $97,762 to raise a newborn to age six.
- A single parent earning $15,900 annually will spend $45,442 to raise a newborn to age six.
- A single parent earning $57,800 annually will spend $101,658 to raise a newborn to age six.

The costs (or expenses) associated with raising a child include: housing, food, transportation, clothing, health care, education and miscellaneous expenses.

There are ways to save on the costs for raising your child. Taxpayers will get a $1,000 tax break per child (up from $500) beginning this year. You can start saving for your child's education at birth. A few common sense things are: Don't go hog-wild on buying baby clothes or furniture. You'll find that children experience a rapid rate of growth during this time in their lives – too many clothes may be wasted because the child could outgrow them before he/she has worn them. You can also join a warehouse club and buy in bulk for your baby.

Additionally, the amount needed to raise a child from birth to age 18 is equally interesting and more expensive. A couple with one child born in 2000, taking in less than $38,000 annually, will spend about $150,330 over 17 years, or about 35% of annual earnings. A couple with a combined annual income of more than $64,000 will spend about 17% of their income, a total of $299,795, by the time the child is 18.

How has your personal income changed since you began living The 90% Rule?

It is because of the Anointed One and His Anointing that I was able to go from depression and debt to empowerment and prosperity. From bankrupt in 1997, my income rose to $50,000 in 1998; in January of 1999, it rose to $60,000; and in August of 1999, it rose to $72,000. By January of 2000, it had risen to $92,000. By September 2001 it became $101,000.

My wife and I give 95% of the contributions received by Carter Ministries – we are blessed to be a blessing. In addition to the offerings we gave to other churches and ministries last year, we gave more than 25% of our income away. Armed with the knowledge and operating by **The 90% Rule**, our family debt is less than 19% of our income, and dropping. We have been able to lower our debt even with the purchase of new cars for our daughters and paying their full college tuition and books. We have been through the pit of poverty but now we're back! It is because we daily fill ourselves with the living Word of God. We didn't seek money; we sought the wisdom of God. And in all our getting, we finally got some financial understanding.

Part of our outreach for Carter Ministries is to assist families in getting control of their debt and obtaining financial freedom. We became our own clients. The first thing we did was to have an independent Financial Needs Analysis performed for us. In this process, we defined our financial goals, identified our total income and expenses and established a timetable for becoming debt-free. We have combined our professional experience as financial consultants with God's anointing of **The 90% Rule**.

Our family objective is to establish a game plan to become debt-free as soon as possible. Our mortgage was an Adjustable Rate Mortgage (ARM). The interest rate had increased every year and we were scheduled to pay it off in June 2022. We looked at several mortgage companies for refinancing opportunities. Few wanted to touch us because of the bankruptcy on my record. We found what we thought was a good deal from a California mortgage company that would have saved us $100 a month on our payments but we would pay more than $340,000 in interest.

We went to the mortgage company that we have an investment account with and saved more than $140,000 in interest and will pay off our new 30-year mortgage in November 2014, seventeen years earlier than our original mortgage. This is possible because we make a payment every two weeks and an extra $50 mortgage payment.

(Remember the "unspecified principal-reduction strategy"?) We were also able to pull $20,000 in equity from our home and liquidate 80% of out credit card and 100% of our installment debts.

What strategies did you use to get your family out of debt?

Dr. Creflo A. Dollar, Jr., gave us the **prayer and faith strategies** that we employ daily. He said that we must have a "point of contact" for our debts, in essence a written declaration that is placed in the container with all of your bills. Ours is as follows:

The Carter's Debt – Free Point of Contact

1. Favor
2. Unexpected Income
3. Debt-releasing Anointing

   "In the name of Jesus, we declare right now that it is the will of the Father that we are debt-free; therefore, we declare my God is a debt-canceling God. He is no respecter of persons, and He wants us out of debt. In the name of Jesus, we put heaven on notice, and we speak our freedom now from the spirit of debt. In the name of Jesus, we receive the anointing for debt release. And in the name of Jesus, we receive the favor for debt release. And in the name of Jesus, we fully expect unexpected income to come our way.

   This paper is my point of contact, and in Jesus' name, when this paper hits our bills, we will release our faith to receive favor, unexpected income, debt cancellation, and

every anointing needed to remove our burdens and destroy our yokes. We declare before heaven and hell this day that we are free from debt. In Jesus' name, debt cancellation begins now!" "*With God all things are possible.*" (Matthew 19:26)

The **practical strategies** we employed to accelerate the pay-off of our debts were as follows:

1. Restructured our debts (rolled most of our consumer debts into a first mortgage)
2. Enrolled in a Mortgage Equity Builder Program and made bi-weekly mortgage payments (using the unspecified principal-reduction strategy)
3. Optimized our debt payments (using a systematic order of debt payment to eliminate smaller amounts first)
4. Established a significant monthly savings account
5. Provided for immediate cash needs and long-term income protection in the event of our untimely death
6. Increased our tithes and offerings to include ministry partnerships
7. Began part-time work as financial consultants for Carter Ministries' Conferences and workshops.

The **spiritual strategies** we employed to accelerate the pay-off of our debts were to add to our daily devotions and pray the biblical basis for the petitions of our heart. In his book, HOW TO GET OUT OF DEBT GOD'S WAY, Dr. Creflo Dollar, Jr., advised us to find a biblical reference for everything that we're asking God for and speak it aloud daily as we pray and meditate on the Word of God.

The Petitions of our (Matthew and Rita Carter) heart to God (each petition begins with "I" because we are one flesh as husband and wife):

- I pray in the anointing: Matthew 6:9-13
- I thank God for the anointing of my ministry with mission: Luke 4:18-19
- I have a worldwide ministry with a mission: Matthew 28:18-20
- I am anointed with wealth and prosperity: Deuteronomy 8:7-9; Malachi 3:10; Luke 6:38; John 10:10
- I have a mind free from worry that is always thinking positive, clean and spiritual thoughts: Philippians 4:8
- I can do all things: Philippians 4:13; 2 Corinthians 4:7-10
- God will supply all of my needs: Philippians 4:19; John 10:10
- I am an anointed husband: Ephesians 5:25-29
- Rita is an anointed wife: Ephesians 5:22-24
- Pearl and Markesha are anointed children: Ephesians 6:1-3
- I pray daily for the household of faith (all believers): Ephesians 6:18
- I have no fear: Romans 8:15
- I am called to preach and teach with power sincerity and truth: Romans 10:13-14
- My body is a living sacrifice and the temple of the Holy Spirit: Romans 12:1
- My mind has been transformed into the mind of Christ: Romans 12:2
- I am anointed with perfect health and longevity of life: Psalms 91:11-16
- I will bless the LORD daily: Psalms 103:1-8

- I will be wise in the use of the finances God has entrusted to me: Proverbs 21:20
- I will not be a borrower: Proverbs 22:7
- Jesus is my friend, closer than a brother: Proverbs 18:24
- I seek first God's kingdom and righteousness therefore, all that I ask for will be given to me: Matthew 6:33
- I believe that Jesus Christ is the Son of the one true and living God and I diligently seek Him daily, therefore, He will reward me with the petitions of my heart: Hebrews 11:6

By using these strategies of **The 90% Rule**, we have been able to accelerate payment of our debts. This year we have a new goal, to be totally debt-free in August, 2007. In five years, everything (including our mortgage) will be paid in full. Now you see why it is so important to set your family's financial goals and re-visit them annually. Just working with what we have, our current salaries and our ministry with a mission, God has granted us the increase!

I am empowered to prosper by the Anointed One and His anointing with wealth and prosperity. I am anointed with the wealth favor of God. I am anointed with the wealth and prosperity to bring God's tithes and my offerings into the House of God. I am anointed to carry the Word of God to the four corners of the world through Carter Ministries. I am anointed to serve as a spiritual distribution center to give offerings to preachers, teachers, evangelists, missionaries and apostles to feed the hungry, clothe the naked, provide shelter for the homeless, to educate the illiterate, to be a blessing to the less fortunate and for the body of Christ to live the abundant life. I will never be broke another day in my life!

BIBLIOGRAPHY

"All debt counselors are not the same," Christine Dugas, *USA Today* (Gannett Co., Silver Springs, MD, May 27, 2002).

The American Heritage Dictionary of the English Language, (Houghton Mifflin Company, Boston, MA, 4th Edition, 2000).

"American seniors rack up debt like never before," Christine Dugas, *USA Today* (Gannett Co., Silver Springs, MD, April 24, 2002).

"Bankruptcy Explosion," Fred A. Schneyer, Business Wednesday, *Tallahassee Democrat(*Tallahassee, FL, Knight-Ridder Newspapers, February 19, 1992).

"Bankruptcy Explosion – More people are choosing it as a way out of financial chaos," Fred A. Schneyer, Business Wednesday, *Tallahassee Democrat* (Tallahassee, FL, Knight-Ridder Newspapers, February 19, 1992).

"Blessed Assurance," Hymn Number 27, The New National Baptist Hymnal (National Baptist Publishing Board, Nashville, TN, 29th Printing, March 1988).

"A Charge To Keep," Hymn Number 190, The New National Baptist Hymnal (National Baptist Publishing Board, Nashville, TN, 29th Printing, March 1988).

"Court rules for credit-reporting agency," Anne Gearan, Associated Press, in the *Tallahassee Democrat* (Tallahassee, FL, Knight-Ridder Newspapers, November 14, 2001).

CREDIT REPAIR & MAKING YOUR FINANCES WORK FOR YOU, Stanley and Melody Harris (Tallahassee, FL, Waters International, 1991).

"Customers can fix errors in their credit reports," Fred A. Schneyer, Business Wednesday, *Tallahassee Democrat* (Tallahassee, FL, Knight-Ridder Newspapers, April 8, 1992).

"Debt smothers America's youth", Christine Dugas, *USA Today* (Gannett Co., Silver Springs, MD, June 20, 2001).

"Getting Off Dead Center," Rev. David Henderson (Jacob Chapel Free Will Baptist Church, April 24, 1994), Nehemiah 2:17-18.

"Greenspan urges financial literacy," Associated Press, in the *Tallahassee Democrat* (Tallahassee, FL, Knight-Ridder Newspapers, October 27, 2001).

Holy Bible, King James Version (Thomas Nelson Publishers, Nashville, TN, 1984).

"HOW MUCH WILL THE BABY COST YOU? The Cost to Raise a Newborn Through Age 5 Has Never Been Higher," Consumer Reports (Yonkers, NY, October 2001).

"How to check out a credit-counseling agency," Christine Dugas, *USA Today* (Gannett Co., Silver Springs, MD, May 27, 2002).

HOW TO GET OUT OF DEBT GOD'S WAY, Dr. Creflo A. Dollar, Jr. (Creflo Dollar Ministries, College Park, GA 1977).

"How Well Do You Hear?" Dr. R.B. Holmes, Jr. (Bethel Missionary Baptist Church, Tallahassee, FL, December 5, 1999), 1 Samuel 3:4-10.

Investing During Your Middle Years, Larry Burkett (Victor Books, Wheaton, IL, 1977).

"IBD's 10 Secrets to Success," *Investor's Business Daily* (Los Angeles, CA, Thursday November 8, 2001).

"Latest Fed move cuts both ways," Barry Flynn, *Orlando Sentinel* (Tribune Publishing Company, Orlando, FL, November 7, 2001).

"The Middle Class: The rules of the economy game are rigged to favor the rich and influential," Donald L. Barlett and James B. Steele, *Philadelphia Inquirer*, in the *Tallahassee Democrat* (Tallahassee, FL, Knight-Ridder Newspapers, November 10, 1991).

"The Middle Class: What Went Wrong," Donald L. Barlett and James B. Steele, *Philadelphia Inquirer*, in the *Tallahassee Democrat* (Tallahassee, FL, Knight-Ridder Newspapers, November 10, 1991).

Minimum Wage to Maximum Wealth, Barbara Martin (Tangible Assets Publications, Oceanside, California, 1990).

Money Cometh! To the Body of Christ, Leroy Thompson (Ever Increasing Word Ministries, Darrow, LA), 5th Printing, 1999.

"Personal Financial Information Report," Primerica Life Insurance Company (Boston, MA, 1997).

Prayers That Avail Much, Word Ministries, Inc. (Harrison House Publishers, Tulsa, OK, Rev. Ed. 1980).

Prosperity Confessions, Carol A. Hunter (Prosperity Unlimited, Inc., College Park, GA, 1998).

PROSPERITY: The Choice Is Yours, Kenneth Copeland (KCP Publications, Fort Worth, TX, Reprinted December, 1990).

Rapid Debt Reduction Strategies, John Avanzini, (HIS Publishing Co., Hurst, TX, Vol. II, 1990).

"Review Your Credit Yearly, Experts say," Fred A. Schneyer, Business Wednesday, *Tallahassee Democrat* (Tallahassee, FL, Knight-Ridder Newspapers, April 8, 1992).

"The Rewards of Research," Carolyn M. Brown, "Black Wealth Initiative" (Black Enterprise Magazine, Earl Graves, Sr., Editor & Publisher, November 2001, Vol. 32, No. 4).

"A Rumbling in their Stomachs," Andrea Stone, Weekend Edition, *USA Today (*Gannett Co., Silver Springs, MD, September 27, 1992).

STEWARD Tips, John Avanzini (International Faith Center, Inc., Ft. Worth, TX, 1997).

A Tale of Two Cities, Large Print Edition, Charles Dickens, (Harper Collins Publishers, London, 1999).

"Ten Reasons Why People Don't Reach Financial Success," Glenn Burkins, *Philadelphia Inquirer*, in the *Tallahassee Democrat* (Tallahassee, FL, Knight-Ridder Newspapers, July 21, 1991).

"Twelfth-Night," William Shakespeare, Act II, Scene V.

"U.S. Population is Mainly Christian," Associated Press, in the *Tallahassee Democrat* (Tallahassee, FL, Knight-Ridder Newspapers, April 11, 1991).

WAR ON DEBT – Breaking the Power of Debt, John Avanzini (HIS Publishing Company, Hurst, TX, Vol. I, 1990).

"What you need to know about credit reports," Fred A. Schneyer, Business Wednesday, *Tallahassee Democrat* (Tallahassee, FL, Knight-Ridder Newspapers, April 8, 1992).

"WorldCom Files for Bankruptcy; Largest U.S. Case", Simon Romero and Riva D. Atlas, *New York Times*, (New York, NY, Monday July 22, 2002).